From demo to limo to God

BOB GRACE

who worked with
Dusty Springfield, David Bowie, Dire Straits
and the Spice Girls – among others

Contents

Acknowledgements

Firstly, I must thank my wife Yvonne, for her love, and robust encouragement to begin, continue and finish writing this book and get it published.

I would also like to thank the following people for their invaluable help.

My daughter Anna, for making me stick to my guns.

My son James, for enduring and filming my talks at book launches.

My elder son Adrian, for his invaluable help in all things digital.

Don Latham for his continual enthusiastic support and guidance.

Nick Battle also for his continual enthusiasitic support.

John Benedict, Music Industry lawyer and friend for his free and valuable advice.

Anna Dimitriadis for the cover art.

Bryn Haworth for being the first person to lead me to Jesus, his music and foreword.

John Irvine, Associate Vicar of Holy Trinity, Cambridge for helping me to establish a firm foundation in Christ back in 1989

Tim and Wendy Wheeldon for their ongoing love, support, proof reading and homemade bread.

Chris Powell, Pete Goddard and all at Verité for putting this book together.

Clive Price, Editor Supremo, (e:mail: office@cliveprice.com) without who this endeavour would not have been possible to complete.

And lastly, The Holy Spirit, for keeping His promise to faithfully help me recall my memories.

Endorsements

"I have worked with Bob on the streets of Bath in helping many a passerby to encounter a Love which is beyond themselves, and to motivate them to start their own journey. What comes to mind as I read this book and think on my own relationship with Bob, is both his enthusiasm to share that Love, intermingled with his own rich treasury of storeys and adventures. They both go together to make up this life giving journey of exploration in the enclosed pages.

Bob has not only searched for, but found what so many people are looking for in all the wrong places. What is it?... well... let the story begin!..."

Paul Skelton
(Founder: Healing On The Streets Bath)

"As one who, for 25 years, chose to bury my head deep in the sand of show-business rather than hear a single word from God, I found reading Bob Grace's book "Rock Solid" utterly compelling - and I believe it will be uplifting and encouraging for any and all readers, not least for the insight it reveals on many aspects of the music industry, and for the fascinating detail about Bob's personal thoughts and feelings along the way. The journey into belief is always interesting; in the case of Grace, it's amazing."

Paul Jones
(Musician/songwriter & broadcaster)

"I have known Bob since the early 70's. He was running Chrysalis Music and I was working with Tony Defries (who was David Bowie's manager at the time). Our friendship continued after he moved to Rondor Music and I started producing for A&M records - working with MIke D'Abo and Cat Stevens. We lost touch when I went back to South Africa for a period, but reconnected when I started Cornerstone Church in Esher in 1990. Since then Bob and I have encouraged each other in our faith.

Bob is a very genuine and honest friend who has a great testimony of how God can suddenly intervene and make a real difference in a person's life. I can recommend this book for anyone who is involved in the entertainment industry. No matter what road you are taking towards your destiny, there is something in it for you!"

Rev. Chris Demetriou

(Founder and Senior Pastor of Cornerstone The Church, Walton - Thames, Surrey, UK.)

"Bob has an electric smile and dynamic personality that lights up any situation. In "Rock Solid" you will find out how a dramatic power encounter with Jesus totally transformed his life. "God hit me like a freight train" he says, and it impacted in a way that could not be experienced through meditation or alcohol.

His personal story and wisdom will totally engage and inspire you to want to know more about how it is possible to find fulfilment in this life and to be assured that there is an even better life to come - and that it is not through reincarnation!"

Don Latham

(Consultant, author, mentor, and International speaker. Founder of MENUNITED men's ministry in Bath)

"Bob Grace was the most talented music publisher of his generation - David Bowie, Supertramp, Dire Straits, Squeeze, were just some of the name artists that Bob signed. When he came to faith in the 90's I was delighted and we became good friends."

Not surprisingly, God threw us together in business not long after and then came "The Spice Girls".

A true gentleman who has looked into the abyss and walked into the light. It is a privilege to call him my friend and I encourage you to read "Rock Solid" and hear Bob's own unique story of God's redeeming love"

Nick Battle

(Author, Broadcaster & Musician)

Rock Solid

Foreword

by Bryn Haworth

I remember watching a TV interview with a band member of Hank Williams, the great country singer-songwriter, who tragically died of drink and drugs at age 30. 'Hank was a man who climbed up a mountain,' said the musician, 'but when he got to the top he found there was nothing there.'

It's a familiar story I've heard many times over the years – not just from the world of music but also from every walk of life. 'There's got to be more to life than this,' is the cry. And thank God, there is.

I first met Bob Grace back in the mid-70s just after being signed as an artist to A&M Records. They recommended I put my songs with Rondor Music, where Bob was managing director. I remember him being a very likeable man – a gentleman – but with a sharp business acumen and, unusually, an open mind. He was pastoral in his dealings with other writers, and was interested in them as people. He brought them together to write with each other.

I've been a professional guitar player since I was 17. I played in bands in England and America, and worked as a session guitarist for many top artists. I survived the 60s and early 70s 'drug fest' which led me to start asking the big questions of life – 'who am I?';' what am I doing here?'; and 'God are you there?'

My wife Sally and I had tried to adjust our lifestyles (just in case there was a God!). We'd stopped doing drugs, drinking, smoking, had become vegetarians and then fruitarians, trying to make ourselves 'pure'. Although we felt better, we still didn't know God, so went back to our old ways.

One June day in 1974, we went for a drive and ended up in what we thought was a circus tent, but which turned out to be a Gospel meeting. We heard about Jesus for the first time, took him at his word and welcomed him into our lives. This obviously effected my songwriting. So as well as composing standard pop songs, now I wanted to communicate Jesus.

Bob was obviously on a search of his own at the time we first met. I remember he always listened very attentively when we talked about Jesus. To give you an idea of how fast things were changing, one week Bob took us out to a fine restaurant for a great steak meal. A couple of weeks later, he came to our home. We'd prepared roast pheasant with all the trimmings and a very expensive claret. As we sat down to eat, he announced he'd become a Hindu, a vegetarian and no longer drank. He manfully picked his way through the vegetables!

I recall another visit a while later when Bob came to our house. Under instruction from the A&M Managing Director, he asked if I could change the lyrics to some of my songs. Understandably, they were struggling with the concept of marketing Jesus' Second Coming! Inevitably after two albums, A&M and I parted ways, and I followed the new roads opening up to me. My problem was I just couldn't keep the 'Good News' to myself.

I lost all contact with Bob. Fifteen years later I was leading worship at a Christian conference with well-known preacher John Wimber (who himself was part of the mainstream music scene before finding faith). I saw this familiar smiling face coming towards the stage. To my delight, Bob told me he'd become a follower of Jesus.

It's been wonderful to see how Bob developed his faith, while still working in the music business. To see him married to the beautiful Yvonne, having fun, enjoying a rich and fruitful life and being a blessing to so many through all the adventures God has led them, makes me feel excited for their future together. There's nothing dull about becoming a Christian!

It's not unreasonable – or surprising – to find creative people looking for their creator. Like other successful people, Bob is a man who's been to the top of the mountain. But unlike many of them, Bob found fire on top of the mountain and is no longer, as Hank Williams sang, on the 'Lost Highway', but is living in the 'Promised Land'.

$\mathcal{O}$ne

Oh What A Lovely War!

$\mathbf{S}$ potting enemy aircraft might sound a noble task. It wasn't. Dad had to endure this solemn and boring duty from a base in Romney Marsh. He was part of the early warning system during World War II. But then his big break came. He was rescued by two brothers, George and Alfred Black. These officers came from a privileged background. They were part of a family that owned a chain of theatres in England at that time, and knew my dad well from his role as an agent. That's theatrical – not secret, by the way! They had been asked by a top brass in the army to organise the entertainment for the troops, and they knew my dad was their man. They 'pulled strings', as he had to be promoted way above his rank to do this job. And so it was that he helped run 'Stars in Battledress'.

When Mum first met Dad – a.k.a Sydney – she wasn't sure what a theatrical agent was. She assumed he worked in a shop that hired out fancy dress. My father had worked his way up from office junior to senior executive in a theatrical agency called Moss Empires. My parents had met while on holiday in Jersey, a popular destination at the time in the 30s. Mum, always the bolder partner, offered to buy him a drink in a hotel bar, and they were smitten. They courted for three years, while living 100 miles apart, as my father first wanted to save up and buy a house for his parents, which he achieved, before getting married and providing another house for his bride. I think Mum was Dad's one and only girlfriend. Moral values were much higher in those days.

And so it was that I was born just after the war, on 31st July 1946, at the Peter Pan nursing home in Angmering-on-Sea in Sussex. I was part of what was named 'The Bulge' at that time. There was a huge increase in the birth rate immediately after the European conflict, with a knock-on effect on teenagers – and parents – in later years. My parents had moved to Sussex to escape war-stricken London, no doubt looking for a little peace of mind. They weren't likely to find it with my emergence! They had experienced a relatively calm arrival of my sister, Virginia, some four years earlier. I had a very lucky escape in the first few weeks on the planet. Apparently they had planned to name me Miles all along, and changed it at the last minute. Apologies, of course, to anyone who answers to the name of Miles. But it wouldn't have worked for me.

Another reason for choosing Angmering was that it was a haven for many show business personalities at that time. An important showbiz mogul had a weekend home there, and he invited many of these artists to house parties. Many famous performers had moved there during the war, and could be found performing on Saturday night at the local pub – much to the amazement of the locals. Many of these new residents were Dad's clients.

When I turned four, we moved to an enormous house in the Hampton Court area. Moving day was the first time I realised I was alive. I remember running round the garden, just experiencing being aware of everything for the first time. The house looked big not just because I was small – but also because it was actually enormous. Named 'Four Winds', as it was located on the corner of a crossroads, it still stands today, but with much of the land sold off for a housing development.

With her lightning-fast mind, Mum had determined by now that her husband was actually an important agent. He was booking exclusively many of the big names in entertainment of the day, such as Alma Cogan, The Crazy Gang and Billy Cotton, famous for his televised band show, with his strap line 'Wakey Wakey'. He also personally managed comedian Arthur Haynes – who the BBC crowned as 'a forgotten king of British TV comedy – and all-round entertainer Roy Castle, who he also discovered, and worked with veteran English-born entertainer Bob Hope. Mum had persuaded Dad to buy this house in keeping with his 'status'. It was perceived to be very important in the 50s to establish your status. It was called 'keeping up with the Joneses'. At any rate, it was very important to Mum, but not so much to Dad.

Having an aversion to mortgages, three years later we moved to a lovely detached – but more modest – abode in New Malden, a suburb of Kingston-upon-Thames, much to Mum's heartbreak. This was the start of my chequered educational career. I was on my third school by the time we moved. I like to joke a little when I introduce my American born wife of nearly 20 years, by saying, 'This is my wife, Yvonne… she's from New York… I'm from New Malden!' My formative days were in this suburban town – which for some peculiar reason I loved – over the ten years that we lived there. The only departure from life in New Malden, was the part of the school holidays when we went to Lyme Regis, where my parents had bought a terraced cottage in the town. I remember being determined to fit in with the local boys, and can still mimic a fine West Country accent to this day. They were obviously puzzled by my London dialect as they nicknamed me 'Fit'. I can only assume they thought I spoke in a mad sort of way!

The local vicar lived next door in the manse. I often wondered why we never saw him or his family, and later found out my parents had scared him off, probably for fear of being evangelised! The church elders lived two houses away, and were very no-nonsense, no make-up, no TV, no fun, and put me off religion a bit. However, a boy my own age, Peter Smithers, lived a few houses the other way, and I went to church with him – mainly for the youth group called YPF (Young People's Fellowship). I was quite a good 'joiner'. Sticking with it was another matter.

I went to the youth group on Fridays, sang in the choir, and went to Sunday school without the support or interest of my parents. They said they wanted to keep an open mind, which was their justification for not going. I must have had some of God's Word in me at that time, as I remember learning Scripture verses for a test while being up in a tree house. An ancient Jewish prophet said God's Word never returns void (Isaiah 55:11), which may in part be an explanation of my turning to the Almighty in later life. To the best of my knowledge, no one was praying for me at that time – with the possible exception of the church leadership. I have to say, I have no recollection of anyone directing me to 'get saved' during those years. Perhaps it wasn't the done thing then!

I went to a private prep school nearby called 'The Study' for a couple of years, and was quite happy. Suddenly, aged nine, I was whisked out with no preparation and sent off to a swanky boarding

The Study

school in Banstead called 'Aberdour'. I was in a state of shock having never been away from home before, and I didn't like it one bit. The rules were so tedious, and the weekends so boring. In those days, boarding meant you stayed there all term with the exception of a half-term break. They had none of the exeat or weekly boarding options that are so prevalent today. Dad even sent someone from his office in his place on sports day, which had the effect of confirming to me the feeling of being abandoned. I made some friends with Lord Teddar's son, and a boy named Lloyd-Bostock. As we all called ourselves by our surnames, as did the teachers, my friends were named respectively, Teddar, and 'Bossy 3' as Lloyd–Bostock had two elder brothers.

I was still pretty miserable there, and longed to return home. The school didn't understand me or I them. For instance, in a bid to be helpful to our form master Mr Cory, who had locked the classroom, and left the key on the inside, I nipped across the headmaster's garden, opened the classroom window, clambered in and got the key. My reward was to be caned for being out of bounds and breaking and entering! There was no justice. I thought if I started to deliberately wet the bed, I would be sent home, so I put this plan into action. To my dismay, my parents' response was to take me to a hypnotherapist in London, Dr Magonet, in an attempt to cure me. That was weird. I remember him saying in a monotone, 'When I snap my fingers, your leg will be as heavy as lead'. And it was. I actually found it hard to break the habit I had deliberately started, and I was given a sort of aluminium undersheet, that sounded a loud buzzer when sodden! That soon snapped me out of it.

> **I thought if I started to deliberately wet the bed, I would be sent home**

This dastardly plan having failed, I resorted to plan B. It was a hanging crime at school to steal anything, so I decided to deliberately steal one or two things, and make sure I was found out.

I took a pair of another boy's swimming goggles and an empty plastic lemon squeezer, and put them in my locker. I then told the school sneak what I'd done, swearing him to secrecy, safe in the knowledge that he would blurt it out for all to hear. Job done. In no time at all, I was apprehended, and I had confessed all to the scary headmaster, Mr Grange, who always wore a kilt, complete with a dirk (dagger) in his sock. He was a sort of 50s Rob Roy. I was duly caned, and asked to leave. What a result!

Mother was put out. The reason for sending me away, I soon determined, was to boost her social profile, as having children at boarding school was very chic. The *actual* education was clearly secondary. Father had no opinion on the matter other than wanting to agree with whatever mother wanted. Raising children was her business, and while loving us kids to bits, he had very little input into raising us. Neither of my parents had much in the way of education. Mother actually thought her children would be better prepared for life without it, as we would have to fight for survival, and be stronger for it. This isn't guesswork. She actually admitted it to me in later years – along with her mistrust of teachers bordering on hatred.

So, in mid term, I found myself at Elm Road Primary School, still aged nine, where my new best friend Johnny's dad was a dustman. This honestly didn't bother me a bit, as I made friends with who I liked as opposed to who they were. However, my mum was definitely not pleased, and repeatedly criticised me for befriending 'the lowest of the low' and for 'kicking me in the teeth for all I've done for you', and so on. Her social climbing agenda was wrecked, and I was the culprit. We sorted things out later on – about 30 years later, to be frank. I remember scraping through the 11 plus exam, not well enough to go to grammar school but to attend a grammar stream in a secondary modern school at Wimbledon, called 'Pelham'. I was quite excited about it, but it didn't go down well on the home front. I lasted about two years there, and realised this wasn't a good situation. I was always in trouble for something, and mother looked quite out of place in her mink coat when inevitably she was called in.

We started looking at more boarding schools. I would have attended Hurstpierpoint in Sussex – save for the unfavourable report from Pelham's headmaster. A good and friendly private day school was next on the plan, called Coombe House, near Kingston. They were probably so desperate for funds they accepted me, and I loved it from day one. I started doing well for the first time academically, learning Russian with a wonderful teacher named Colonel Jerome, and doing well in most other subjects, staying in the top five of the class or better.

> **I knew no matter how hard I tried, my voice was croaky**

I was a fast long distance runner – something positive I'd taken from Pelham. And with the able assistance of our much loved sports master Mr Cherry, I even went on to participate in county events such as cross country running. I made some really good friends there. But my own musical aspirations had to stay distinctly amateur. I had no problem about that. I knew no matter how hard I tried, my voice was croaky.

I wasn't going to be a star. But I was going to make some.

Coombe House

Rock Solid

T**W**O

Dance On

Despite my lack of musical prowess, I joined a local band. 'The Conchords' took me on as rhythm guitarist, as I was able to play all my favourite Shadows songs – among others. The Shadows were the pop heroes of the day. They also backed Cliff Richard, the Brit 'Elvis'. There was very little rock music as such in Britain – it was Cliff and The Shadows who'd helped bring rock 'n' roll to these shores. And as far as I was concerned, I was their number one fan. I strived in vain to play as well as lead guitarist Hank B Marvin. But eventually I settled to emulate Bruce Welch, the band's brilliant rhythm guitarist and songwriter. I even went as far as getting the same instrument – a Fender Stratocaster – from the same shop, Jennings of Charing Cross Road, London.

I was aided in this endeavour by David Bryce, a business friend of Dad's. He actually worked for The Shadows as their tour manager, and later went on to work exclusively for Cliff in a similar capacity. One of Dad's management clients was Dickie Valentine, England's answer to Johnny Ray in the early 60s, and David was Dickie's brother. There's nepotism at work for you! I got to meet The Shadows and Cliff loads of times, as their manager – the late, great Peter Gormley – was another good friend of Dad's. I remember pestering Bruce Welch on how to play the chords of their hit record FBI, and was honoured by attending the recording session of the single *Atlantis*.

| **I got to meet The Shadows and Cliff loads of times**

I had to almost hold my breath on the 'take' as I was sitting next to them on the studio floor. What a buzz!

My other passions included making model aeroplanes that actually flew, and cycling. I thought nothing of riding to the seaside and back the same day. My parents refused to let me buy anything on HP – short for 'Hire Purchase'. So I used to work a paper round, and toil in factory canteens and supermarkets in the school holidays, to get the money together to buy the parts to build 'superbikes'. The frame was a classic 'Carpenter' and anything else I could lay my hands on was by the Italian manufacturer Campagnolo. Basically, my parents would contribute 50 per cent to projects they approved of and I was saving for, and I found it to be a both fair and a good incentive to work. Plus as I had such long school holidays, I grew bored with just hanging around.

I had a friend locally named Julian Legg, who I remember as being very bright academically, and also very strong as he boxed for his school. He had an elder sister named Jan, who was secretary to Eric Easton, first manager of The Rolling Stones. She thought they were 'super' and cajoled me and Julian to check them out, as they played regularly in nearby Kingston and Richmond. I was already familiar with gigs in Kingston, as I used to go out regularly with my best friend Barry Austin to jazz concerts at the Coronation Baths Hall and various music venues. Not that jazz interested me at all, but the support bands were invariably pop groups in the Cliff and Shads vein.

> **Experiencing The Rolling Stones in person was 'mind-blowing**

But experiencing The Rolling Stones in person was, as they say – 'mind-blowing' – and I became an avid fan. The great thing was that you could talk to them before and after the show as it was very early on in their career. I would chat regularly with Brian Jones about guitar and harmonica techniques. I remember bumping into him in Regent Street, London, when he directed me to a shop were he bought his harmonicas – Scarth, in Charing Cross Road. I have to confess I found the instrument confoundingly difficult and soon dropped it. The Stones' scruffy appearance and radical musical departure from The Shadows made it tough for me to retain my status as the Shads' number one fan – which I felt a little guilty about – but c'est la vie! I kept on at my dad to sign them, but it wasn't his world. I always felt good about 'spotting them' early on, even trying to order an album before they had a record deal. Little was I to know then, being a talent scout was going to be my career.

My sister Virginia got married at this time, to a Ugandan Asian called Hafeez. It took my parents a week or so to come to terms with her marrying this chap. But we all came to love him, even if he did whisk her off to Kampala for seven years. They returned to the UK to escape the country when Idi Amin started to commit atrocities over there. Virginia and Hafeez had three daughters – Sophia, Yasmin and Marisa – now lovely young women, living in England with their own families. Virginia re-married some time after her daughters left home, to a former police sergeant named John who was a widower. They live in a picturesque part of Norfolk. We all love John to bits.

I celebrated my 16th birthday, left school, and started out on my first career as a travel agent, which was to be short lived. I used to work at an agency called Albany Travel in Cork Street, Mayfair, during school holidays. It seemed a natural transition to go full time. Life was pretty good at the time, as I earned a staggering £5 per week – which amazingly went a long way in 1962 – even if I did sometimes make more from playing with the band. I worked hard, even having to turn up on Saturday mornings which was a little tough, but I don't remember complaining. What did cause me some grief, was noticing the details of the boss's pay packet, which inadvertently he'd left on his desk. This guy was reckoned to be the best in the business without exception, and his wages looked disastrously small to my mind. My incentive to be a travel agent waned at that moment, and I began to consider my position, as they say. I found out that travel agents' commission from airlines was less than say the commission for theatrical agents, so no wonder they got paid less. Plus, I was getting a little hacked out for writing out tickets to exotic places *for other people*. I wanted to find a job where I could travel as well.

Enter the well-known actors' agent Robin Fox – father of Edward and James – who both became film stars at that time. Again, my good old dad had put feelers out for me, and found out that Robin needed an office boy. His agency, London Management, was a division of the Grade Organisation, where my Dad worked and was also a director. It was even in the same building, Regent House, Regent Street, but on a different floor. I had to file all the scripts, and run errands for all the staff and their celebrity clients.

I remember regularly having to deliver things to the actress Sarah Miles, who was engaged to James Fox at that time. She had an enormous white Pyrenean Mountain dog named Addo Le Fontenoy, which I had to walk sometimes. She was a terrific lady, always kind to me, with none of the star ego, and swore like a trooper! James Fox was a star at that time, due to a film he appeared in with Dirk Bogarde and Sarah called *The Servant*. The agency obviously had much control over the film as almost their whole roster of clients got parts, even walk-ons. They also represented the film's director, Joseph Losey.

> I remember regularly having to deliver things to the actress Sarah Miles

James' brother Edward, however, was unknown at that time, but was plying his craft in stage productions held in theatres on Sundays, when such establishments were 'dark'. He was also very kind, and went on to become a huge star, notably as the assassin in *The Day Of The Jackal* in 1973 – which was based on the novel of the same name by Frederick Forsyth. My immediate boss, a lovely lady named Ros Chatto, was absolutely passionate about her job. She clearly adored what she did, her clients, and the world of luvvies that she lived in. My problem was that I wasn't passionate about this world. There was obviously potentially more money in it than being a travel agent, but my passion was for music. My boss asked what I was most excited about and my answer was Fender Stratocasters – an answer which meant absolutely nothing to her, but everything to me.

I was 'poached' by another agency, who represented the comedians Max Bygraves and Barbara Windsor of *Carry On* fame, where I worked for a short while. But then I landed the 'office boy job' of my dreams. I started working in an agency that represented pop stars and rock 'n' rollers – Tito Burns. I had arrived.

Rock Solid

Three

Ticket To Ride

Beatlemania had struck. The latest batch of school-leavers in our part of Surrey descended on a pub called the *Wheatsheaf*. That was the local Mecca for party information and for where guys could meet girls. I absolutely loved every minute of this new world. My parents were not pub types, preferring the odd drink at home or at cocktail parties. So from then on I was out almost every night in this new social whirl – going to instant parties fuelled by beer and Beatles. I was about eighteen, the year was 1964, and it was rockin'.

My work at the Tito Burns Agency was in stark contrast to that of most of my new friends, who were training for so-called 'proper jobs' like law, accountancy, insurance and so on. The conflict I had was that for most people in showbiz, that was their only world. They were totally immersed in it both socially and professionally. One thing was the hours. It wasn't a nine-to-five job most of the time – unlike my friends, whose lives were regulated by train timetables. I never knew where I would be, or what I would be doing from one day to the next. I was the assistant to Tito himself, a former bandleader who ran his company like an army drill sergeant. What he said, went!

The agency often brought American stars over to England to tour, and inevitably they'd have a record released to coincide with the visit. Tito would book prestigious TV shows for them, and if no one else was around, yours truly would have to accompany them.

Dionne Warwick, The Isley Brothers and The Shangri-Las were just some of the American singers I had to chaperone to television stations. These stations weren't just in London, so I'd spend hours travelling up and down the motorways visiting cities like Glasgow, Manchester, and Birmingham.

> **Dionne Warwick and The Shangri-Las were just some I had to chaperone**

Dusty Springfield was a huge star in England. And besides the agency representing her, Dusty's own manager Vic Billings also based his office with us. Due to my work with the agency artistes, I became trusted to accompany Dusty to some TV shows and became very friendly with her. So often in my experience, the biggest stars were the nicest. She was very sweet, and loved to have lots of fun. The parties at her flat in Baker Street were legendary, and I attended many of them. They were pretty wild affairs. One of the most popular pieces was filling the bath with a mixture of water, vinegar, soap powder – in fact, almost anything to hand – and dunking the odd random guest. Dropping chocolate cakes and trifles out of the windows into passing open-top cars was another speciality. Friends from home couldn't believe it until I took one of them along as my guest to prove it!

The wild parties were something of a veneer. For underneath it all, Dusty was very insecure about her own singing ability, so I would encourage her about her uniqueness.

Another big weekly event was the Friday night TV programme *Ready Steady Go*. It was a live show with an audience (even if the performers did all mime to their records!). Producer Vicki Wickham was great friends with Dusty and Vic, so I was able to go every Friday. I mixed with the top stars of the day, like The Beatles and the Stones. This was the hottest ticket in town, and I didn't even realise it! Many elements of the job were great. However, I was still the lowest on the totem pole. I wanted to travel higher in my music industry career.

My goal was to work for a record company. I'd met many such executives at the TV stations, so I applied to a couple of labels for work. One of them was Pye Records, a very successful label in the early 60s based in Marble Arch. I got the standard reply letter.

'Thanks,' they said, 'but nothing going at the moment. We'll keep you on file.'

A few months later, I was having dinner with Dad in a showbiz restaurant, The White Elephant Club. Pye's head of A&R (department responsible for signing artists), Les Cox, came over to chat with Dad. I was duly introduced. Never being backward about going forward, I asked him if there were any jobs. He said write in and so on. I promptly told him I'd already done all that. So he said to ring him. Basically, a few weeks later, I started as a clerk in what was called 'production control' – for the princely wage of £12 per week. Not much, I admit – but I was in! This was still a nine-to-five job, overseeing the transition of the manufacture of the record.

Frankly, it became a bit boring. However, another new boy had started at the same time as me, named Peter Sonter, in the promotion department – and what he told me about his job was definitely up my street. He would complain to me in the pub that he would have to work all hours, socialising with artists and media executives, going to TV shows, working weekends. That sounded perfect to me. After all, that's what I knew best. I quickly found out he earned exactly the same money as me. I persuaded him it was in his best interest for us to swap jobs. I presented the situation to the much feared boss, Louis Benjamin. Instantly, he recognised it cost him nothing to have two much more productive workers.

It was the swinging 60s and all that went with it – Carnaby Street and Mary Quant

Life as the youngest member of the promotion department was great. It was the swinging 60s and all that went with it – Carnaby Street fashion led by such designers as Lord John and

Mary Quant, girls in mini skirts, and pop music exploding all over the place. And I was at the centre of it. My job was to persuade radio and TV producers to play our company's records and book our artists on their shows. We released about 15 records a week – some of them complete rubbish – but others that went on to be classics.

We were involved with launching the careers of such artists as The Searchers *(Sugar And Spice)*, The Kinks *(You Really Got Me, Lola, Waterloo Sunset)*, Donovan *(Catch The Wind, Hurdy Gurdy Man, Mellow Yellow)* Sandie Shaw *(There's Always Something There To Remind Me, Girl Don't Come)*, Petula Clark *(Downtown)* and countless others.

We used to throw parties for the media – sometimes in our boardroom – to launch new artists and welcome visiting singers and musicians from the USA, who'd naturally have a record to promote. On one occasion, I was sent off to the Hilton Hotel to bring James Brown back to the office for the party to promote his single *Papa's Got A Brand New Bag Part One*. The party started at six o'clock and finished about 7.30. I called for James about five o'clock, to find he wasn't ready – his hair was still being coiffeured! With the monstrous size of his ego, it was pretty tough to explain to him that as important as he was, the British media were more interested in a free drink and getting home.

Eventually I managed to cajole him into going – but not until he'd shared with me the facts of life, something that was surely my father's job! And so it went on at Pye – another week, another record to promote. What a life. I was paid to party. I was worse for wear one afternoon, after a liquid lunch with a radio producer and a well known disc jockey. But unlike other occupations, there was no official reprimand. My boss was pleased I'd been out fulfilling the requirements of my job!

Elizabeth Cowley, producer of a top BBC TV pop music programme called *A Whole Scene Going*, approached me to participate. She wanted to set up a panel of teenagers to interview artists also appearing on the show. She favoured me, as she realised I already knew quite a few of the artists she was booking, such as Dusty Springfield. I'd appeared live once on television before, on a Southern TV show entitled *Disc Quiz* produced by the flamboyant Mike Mansfield, and hosted by the lovely Muriel Young. I'd quite enjoyed the experience, so I said yes to Elizabeth. As this was one of the most sought after shows on British TV to showcase talent, my company Pye Records bent over backward to encourage me, giving me Wednesday afternoon off to do the show.

The live action was most daunting. Sitting on the set at 6.30 on Wednesday evenings, and knowing I'd have to interview singers in front of a live audience of a few million, was a pressure I didn't enjoy. When the moment arrived, the floor manager would get down on one knee a few feet away, lift up his hand, and count down with his fingers… 'five-four-three-two-one… you're on!' While quite enjoying the mini-celebrity status among my friends and family, and the occasional member of the public, secretly I dreaded going each week.

The stress of it all didn't diminish. The producers were hoping I would challenge some of the artists I interviewed with some of their darker secrets I knew about. But after consulting with Dad, I refused to co-operate. Eventually I swapped places on the panel with an up-and-coming DJ Mike Quinn, who I knew from Carnaby Street where he used to manage a Lord John shop. I was relieved. I started to think about pastures new.

The breakthrough came in the person of Norrie Paramor, the man who discovered and recorded Cliff Richard, The Shadows and Helen Shapiro. He approached me with the idea of leaving Pye, and working in the promotion department at EMI with a special responsibility to push all the records he produced. Being the former No1 fan of The Shads, how could I refuse – especially with a salary increase to £20 per week?

It was 1965, a special year for music. The Beatles released *Revolver* – an album that shook us all with its experimental approach. It was a stunning range of sounds, from the whimsical *Yellow Submarine* to the nightmarish *Tomorrow Never Knows*. The Beach Boys, another favourite group of mine, released *Pet Sounds* – which has been

> **The Beatles released *Revolver* – The Beach Boys released *Pet Sounds***

described as one of the most influential records in the history of pop. It brought the world such classic tracks as *Good Vibrations* and *God Only Knows*. Interestingly, the latter became known as one of the first pop songs to carry 'God' in the title. They were ground-breaking LPs. Music was changing again. I had the honour of taking these records to radio – obviously not a particularly difficult job. The task was more about making sure the records all arrived with media producers simultaneously to avoid accusations of favouritism – although I did sneak an advance copy of Revolver to an important producer. Everyone wanted 'the exclusive' preview. These days, new albums by superstars are intensely controlled by the labels and artist managements. The consequences are serious for anyone 'leaking tracks'.

By this time, I'd accompanied my parents on a trip to Australia, Singapore, Hawaii and New York – and I got the travel bug. So I decided to leave not only EMI, but also the UK in search of fun, travel and adventure. Initially, I wanted to go to America, as I'd desired to live there for many years. I used to love American products like the *Daisy* airgun, the TV crime drama *Dragnet*, crazy-looking bicycles and clothes. However, the work permit issues – coupled with America's war in Vietnam – closed that option.

The trip to Australia had a big impact on me. It resulted in a job proposal which was exciting – even though it was a little out of the ordinary. One of Dad's clients, Mick Edgley, was a vaudeville performer before the war, with an act called Edgley & Dawe.

After the war, Mick had immigrated to Australia, and came up with the idea of touring the Russian Ballet throughout the island continent. At that time, Russia was locked into the Cold War with the West, so it was quite a bold move. It turned out to be very successful.

The Russians even trained Mick's daughter, Christine, to be a high wire artist, allowing her to tour with them. I was invited to immigrate to Australia (the only way to get a work permit) and go on the road with the troupe. There was also talk of bringing the Russian Circus in as well, so it sounded great. Who didn't want to run away and join the circus?

So, bristling with enthusiasm, I went off to Australia House. Emigration papers were very easy to obtain in 1966. You just paid £10 towards the travel costs called 'assisted passage'. As I was leaving the building with all the documents in my hand, I was approached unofficially by a young civil servant. He asked me if I was emigrating. I responded positively with my circus story. He then asked if I'd been informed that Australia was about to enter the Vietnam conflict, which I hadn't. Basically he said if I emigrated, I would have been in his words, cannon fodder… London-Sydney-Hanoi! The Australian dream in tatters, I pressed on with my determination to live abroad for a while, and came up with Canada. It bordered the USA, was pretty similar to me (though not in Canadians' minds, as I found out), was easy to emigrate to, and had no intention of fighting the North Vietnamese.

An unofficial 'uncle' of mine was Sir Lew Grade

An unofficial 'uncle' of mine was Sir Lew Grade. He was brother of Leslie, my Father's boss at the Grade Organisation. Sir Lew (later Lord Grade) – or Mr Lew to me – had started commercial television in this country, with Pye Records a subsidiary. His office was on the top floor of the same building as Pye. There were two lifts, one for Sir Lew and his fellow directors, and the other one for everyone else. We were strictly forbidden to use the 'Directors Only' lift.

However, I was lingering in the corridor by the lifts one day, when the directors' doors opened and there going down was Sir Lew. Instinctively, I hopped in and reminded him of my status as his 'nephew'. By the time we reached the ground floor, I had the promise of a letter of recommendation to facilitate work in Canada. That was quick work.

A week later, I popped back to his office. As promised, the letter was waiting for me. Showbusiness can often be a very brutal world, darkened even more by some shady characters. But the integrity shown by both Lew and Leslie Grade in all their business dealings was always of the highest character, as far as my family and I could observe through the years.

Some weeks later, I found myself at Liverpool docks, waiting to board *The Empress Of Canada* for the five-day voyage to Montreal.

Four

Summer Of Love

I t was great fun on the boat to Canada. The purser put all the teenagers together – about a dozen in all – and we ate and hung out. Reality crept in when arriving in Toronto, where I had decided to live. I had to first find somewhere to stay that night. I felt a little like Dick Whittington, who believed the promise that the streets of London were paved with gold.

Toronto was cold, and I didn't know a soul

Toronto was cold, the part of town I was in was quite shabby, and I didn't know a soul. I found a boarding house, where the 'kindly' landlady took a week's rent off me in advance. I was shown to a twin bedded room, just happy to dump my belongings at last. I spent that evening with some American boys visiting from Syracuse, New York, and went to bed early, exhausted.

I had a real shock the following morning when I swung my feet round the bed, and put them down not on the floor but on someone's stomach! The canny landlady had rented out the floor of the bedroom to backpackers, and there were about eight people now in the room, sleeping on either side and at the foot of the beds. Even though I'd paid in advance, I vowed to find alternative accommodation by nightfall. Scanning the wants ads in the local paper, I rented a room in a house at Spadina, the Italian sector of Toronto. So far, so good, as I had a little money to get by for a few weeks.

Armed with my letter from Sir Lew, I made an appointment to see his contact in Toronto, Mr Hershel Harris, head of a TV station.

They had nothing going there on the job front, with the same reasons that I would begin to hear a lot – 'no Canadian experience'. Well, how do you get any without that first job? Fortunately, I landed on my feet – at least for a while. Hershel recommended me to Broadcast Music Canada, a branch of a giant US performing rights chain.

Basically performing right societies are non-profit making companies that collect on behalf of members, who are songwriters and publishers, for the monies earned for songs being broadcast on television, film, radio and so on. BMI Canada was looking for a PR (public relations) person to promote awareness over rival organisation CAPAC to radio station bosses. I'd never done PR as such before, but had a sense of what was required due to my time working in the UK record companies.

I bought an English car. It was an MGB open top sports car, which was my first mistake. I didn't grasp exactly how cold the Canadian winter can be. However, I earned a good salary, well over the average for new arrivals, plus they paid me ten cents a mile to drive to these radio stations to begin my charm offensive. When I was a little short, which was most of the time, I would select station a couple of hundred miles away to maximise the mileage offer.

By this time, I had moved into what was called a duplex – a flat with both upstairs and downstairs. By pure chance, at a barbecue I'd met an old school friend, Mike Faulkner from my days at The Study in New Malden. He was off to work in Memphis. But the good news was that he nominated me as his replacement in a lively flat in a good part of Toronto. It was great to be plugged in to a social network, with plenty of parties and new friends. Additionally, a pal from England also moved to Toronto, Rick Smerdon, and he still lives there today.

About nine of us chipped in 100 dollars each. We rented a summer cottage on the shores of Lake Simcoe – where everyone seemed to spend weekends in the summer water skiing, swimming, having barbecues and hosting great parties. You had to be 21 in Canada to drink those days, and prove it with solid ID.

I managed to obtain the birth certificate of a 21-year-old Brit returning to England, so for much of the time I had to pretend to be an individual named Malcolm Hod, which was a little strange. The same group of friends also got together and rented a ski lodge in a resort called Rainbow Ridge. It's a very Canadian 'thing' to have floodlit skiing. It was a wonderful way to spend Saturday night with a few runs down the mountain, sustained by a glass of hot mulled wine.

While Canada was a great place to live, with superb outdoor recreational facilities, it was pretty mundane in 1966 in terms of the music industry. With the swinging 60s in full flow in England, and glorious music coming from America's west coast, in the year before 'The Summer Of Love' in '67, I began to think of returning to London to pursue my ambitions. I quit working as BMI, as they considered I was a little too wild for them, and worked as a clerk at the Bell Telephone Company for a short while, then lastly at the Bulova Watch Company. The last job was really good, and if I didn't have the music 'bug', I would've stayed there without a doubt.

I was putting a few feelers out in England, and kept my relationships intact with my media contacts by sending them all postcards from time to time. EMI offered me my old job back, which I accepted in a heartbeat. One year after arriving in Canada, I found myself in New York, waiting to board the boat *The France*. I chose this one, destination Southampton, as it boasted the longest bar afloat! A week later, I was back home in Surrey, scoping out the job situation.

Despite having a written offer on headed notepaper, the EMI job didn't materialise. The department head who offered the job had the cheek to suggest I was being naive to believe it! His own career was itself short lived, not surprisingly to me. I trawled through a mental list of contacts, and remembered a man called Roger

Welch with whom I'd been in contact during my time at EMI. The brother of wartime singer Vera Lynn, he worked in the music publishing division of United Artists films. He would ring me from time to time always with the same proposition. He offered to lighten my load by doing the radio promotion of soundtrack albums that he published.

All I had to do was give him at no charge my promotional allocation of 25 albums, and he would do the rest. I must say, he got great results as he had developed close relationships with his contacts. He explained to me that music publishers earned good money any time a song was played on the radio or TV, and this was a great way of developing income. I pondered over this whole scenario, and came up with an idea I thought would be beneficial to all concerned.

By this time his company was putting out many pop songs, and my media contacts were very strong in this area. Roger recognised – with some prompting from me – that I could make the company more money than it would cost to hire me through this additional income from performance income. Following a meeting with him, and the company's managing director Noel Rogers, I started immediately at £25 per week.

They operated from a very smart apartment in Knightsbridge, overlooking Hyde Park. But the actual office space was quite limited, and I literally shared Roger's desk and phone – when he wasn't on it. I learned a huge amount from him. He was one of the most industrious workers I had come across at that time. He was the last remnant of the old school of publishers that usually operated from a small street off the Charing Cross Road called Denmark Street, or most commonly 'Tin Pan Alley'. This name was apparently attributed to the cacophony of sound of numerous pianos being played simultaneously, and became the generic term for the music industry for many years – just as 'The Rag Trade' is for fashion.

All sorts of acts – from big bands to jazz trios – performed live on the radio with featured singers. These artists worked hand in hand with music publishers to obtain the 'hot' new songs from the army of songwriters that evolved to meet this demand. It was a very competitive market, with publishers chasing established singers to sing their tunes, and vice versa. The writers would play and sing their songs live to the bandleaders and singers in their company offices.

As singers wanted to go from publisher to publisher to find the best songs, Denmark Street became established as the place to operate from, with hundreds of little companies in operation there. The legendary music publisher Dick James met with The Beatles' manager Brian Epstein in Denmark Street's café *The Giaconda*, and made the deal to represent the Fab Four – as they were called at the time. Dick was a former singer himself, crooning his way through *The Ballad Of Davy Crockett*, and *Robin Hood,* the signature themes from the popular TV series. I sat next to him many years later at an awards ceremony lunch, and asked him if he knew my father.

'Knew him?' he said. 'He was my agent!'

Publishers would also strive to get their songs performed by the bandleaders who had regular radio shows, as this generated performance income. The original hit parade comprised a list of the bestselling sheet music that week. Most homes in England had a family member who could play an instrument. People would listen to the radio broadcasts and then buy their favourite songs to play at home.

Printed sheet music normally had a picture of the singer or bandleader who performed the song and sold in thousands, generating royalty income for the publishers and songwriters. As the technology developed, recording studios started, with many located in Denmark Street, usually in the basement, so publishers could record the songs – or demos as they were called – to play to singers at different locations.

One of those studios, Regent Sound, was where the Rolling Stones recorded their first album. They'd been at a pub in Denmark Street prior to recording the track *Can I Get A Witness*. Mick Jagger obviously hadn't been to the loo – as demonstrated at the end of this track when he wailed, 'Can I get a witness, gotta have a pee'. Check it out. When later, records – as opposed to sheet music – made up the 'Hit Parade', the Music Publishers Association freaked out,

> **Mick Jagger obviously hadn't been to the loo**

predicting these new fangled records would destroy the industry. Naturally, it did put a few printers out of work. I know because I've read the notes of MPA meetings at that time chronicling the events. This event gives me hope for the current future of the industry, which has been ripped apart in many ways due to possibilities presented by the Internet.

Working with Roger was a unique opportunity to catch one last glimpse of the Tin Pan Alley world. I would go with him to the Joe Loss show. Joe was a bandleader with still a very popular live lunchtime radio programme. Amazingly, there was a guest spot for rock bands to play, such as the Stones. So I would get to hang out with the bands afterwards in the nearby pub, while Roger was chatting up Joe Loss or his singers to perform our songs. Hosted by Tony Hall, the show was a hangout place for the industry, and I made many firm friendships there which went on to last a lifetime. He also demonstrated how to get singers to record songs published by our company, called song plugging.

Parent company UA was about to release the film *Chitty Chitty Bang Bang* starring Dick van Dyke. Roger's task was to get as many of the songs in the film score recorded by as many people as possible to generate both income and wider public awareness of the film. Impressively, he got about 18 different recordings – called 'cover versions' – including one by Val Doonican, a very big artist at that time.

Not to be excluded, I got one significant cover with The Shadows, who I'd heard were about to record an album of movie themes. They were performing at the Palladium at that time, and I managed to get five minutes of their time backstage. I presented each one of them with the Dinky Toy duplicate of the Chitty car – and of course the album – resulting in them including a cover of the main title song on their LP.

While the building in Knightsbridge was very 'vibey', in a great location, UA had run out of space. And the head honchos in New York wanted us to share a new, fancy building, with the film company and their record label, UA Records. So it was goodbye to Hyde Park, and our music industry neighbours like Shel Talmy, producer of The Kinks, and Bunny Lewis, manager of many famous 60s disc jockeys – such as David Jacobs – and off to the less salubrious climes of Oxford Street.

Rock Solid

Five

Moving On Up

I had my own fancy office. It was on the ground floor of Mortimer House, the new home for the giant United Artists Corporation in the UK early in 1968. My corner was occupied solely by the music publishing division, and my title was 'Professional Manager'. This was a term that originated from the sheet music days, as sheet music was often referred to as 'professional copies'. In fact, my job was still to get radio play on our catalogue of songs, but now the job description was expanded to sign new writers to the company.

Prior to The Beatles, singers and groups usually performed material written by other people. Post-Beatles, that situation changed dramatically as the Fab Four were also recognised for their prodigious songwriting ability. They even wrote hits in their spare time at the beginning of their success for others such as Billy J. Kramer with *Do You Wanna Know A Secret*, Peter and Gordon's *A World Without Love* and notably, the Rolling Stones with *I Wanna Be Your Man*.

> **It became 'uncool' not to write your own material**

It became 'uncool' – a serious transgression in the 60s – not to write your own material. That resulted in fewer opportunities for publishers to get songs recorded for their roster of songwriters. Recognising this sea change, I became more of a talent scout, looking to sign the songwriting rights of emerging rock bands to the company.

The first, and only, band I signed to UA Music was a Scottish outfit called The Scots of St James, who in later years changed their name to The Average White Band. My instincts were good in spotting the talents of group leader Alan Gorrie, but my timing was a bit off. However, I started the habit of getting out and about in the evening among the music clubs in London. In the process of embracing and mixing with people in this environment, my sphere of contacts was rapidly increasing. This was essential in the music biz as 'what you know and who you know' was a vital combination.

UA was becoming quite a happening company itself, obtaining the exclusive publishing rights to the musical *Hair*, which was a huge success. It was hugely controversial at the time due to dramatically exposing the lack of communication between the generations of the day, and touching on politics, religion and sex. The show also featured a famous nude scene involving the whole cast. You still often hear these songs today, embedded in TV commercials for a variety of products. They also developed the pop side of their label UA Records, which had previously been used more for film soundtracks. They made a big impact with Peter Sarstedt, with his classic *Where Do You Go To My Lovely*. John Paul Jones,

Another regular at the office was Mike Batt of The Wombles

later to be the bass player in Led Zeppelin was often in the building, as he was the musical arranger for French singer Francoise Hardy, whose songs we published at that time. Another regular at the office was Mike Batt, the singer/songwriter/arranger who later went on to enjoy huge success with his project The Wombles.

Commuting from Surrey was becoming a real problem due to the hours I was keeping, and the difficulties of getting home at midnight or later. The trains finished running by 11.30, and driving was out due to a combination of onerous parking charges in London, and the introduction of the breathalyser. Most of my work involved quite a bit of drinking, and I didn't want to lose my driving licence.

The problem was solved when my best friend in the music business, Derek Green, located a three-bedroom flat in Shepherd's Market, a quaint touristy area behind London's Hilton Hotel. The rent was only £11 per week – less than the cost of parking a car. As I had access to better references, it was decided I would be responsible for the lease. So I had the choice of bringing in a third person to share. His name was Tim Knight, a former trainee stockbroking friend from Surrey, who I had helped get into the music industry. By now he also worked at UA, in the record company, and was responsible for their artists' radio and TV promotion.

So there we were, three guys all in the same business, sharing a flat at London's West End in the swinging 60s. We were all instructed by our respective companies to 'network' – and we had expense accounts to fund it. Essentially, I immersed myself in the music business lifestyle, working all hours – seven days of the week sometimes – and rarely had a night off in two years. By pooling our contacts, my flatmates and I seemed to know virtually everyone worth knowing. For example, there was the ritual of attending the live recording of the massively successful TV show *Top Of The Pops* every Thursday evening.

We socialised with the pop stars of the time, along with their friends, managers, agents and hangers-on, in the BBC bar. We also organised a post-show party every Thursday at a friend's flat in Sloane Street, which became the place to go when the BBC bar closed. On other nights of the week, clubs such as The Speakeasy, Bag O' Nails, and The Revolution were our stomping grounds. Due to our involvement with record companies, we had honorary membership to them all. These clubs were a refuge for stars at that time, so we'd be rubbing shoulders – sometimes literally – with people like John Lennon or Jimi Hendrix.

One day Derek and I were attending the opening of a radio station in Liverpool. We were chatting to some local girls in the hotel lobby later that night. Being lads, we were trying to impress them with tales of the stars we knew in London. They asked if we knew Jimi Hendrix. Of course, we responded, as you do, as if he was a lifelong friend. At that very moment, who should enter the hotel lobby but Jimi himself! I must admit, this threw me into a bit of a panic, but Derek managed to control his composure. As Jimi walked by, Derek jumped up and hugged him, greeting him like a long lost friend. Smiles all round, girls introduced, and situation rectified! Derek later told me that like me, he only had a nodding acquaintance with Jimi. But Derek figured correctly, that by that time of night, Jimi would be pretty high on illegal substances and probably wouldn't even recognise his own mother!

I was headhunted early in 1969 to establish the music publishing side of the successful management company Chrysalis. The label was a witty blend of the founder's names Chris Wright and Terry Ellis. I'd met Terry a couple of years previously when he was promoting a tour with Francoise Hardy, and travelled back to London with him after the show. He was very 'straight' back then, with neat hair, suit and so on, and had just left university. He had been social secretary there, and had been involved with booking rock bands for the college. Chris had been fulfilling a similar function at his university. They had both started managing a rock group themselves, Terry with Jethro Tull, and Chris with Ten Years After.

The summer of love the previous year in America had ushered in a new flavour of rock music – named 'underground'. This had really caught on by now, culminating in the Woodstock Festival in August 1969 where 'underground' became mainstream. Ten Years After made an enormous impression on the American public at Woodstock, and Terry and Chris guided their respective bands to international superstardom at this time. Chrysalis had obtained the music publishing rights of both bands, plus other newer bands in the pipeline.

My new job was to set up the publishing company, arrange collection of the global royalties being generated, and try to build the company by discovering some bands and songwriters myself. Terry's appearance had dramatically changed since I had last seen him. You couldn't tell him apart from the rock stars of the day – with hair down to his waist and colourful flower-power clothes. I felt very 'out of place' with my neat hair, tie and mohair suit, which had previously been standard music industry 'uniform'.

However, I took to this new world like a duck to water. To the consternation of some friends – and naturally my parents – I started wearing my hair long with rock 'n' roll clothes. I'd always wanted to run a company, and now I was well and truly in the deep end. Chrysalis was hugely successful, and I entered a steep learning curve of every aspect of the business. I went to an international conference for the first time.

I was besieged with foreign music publishers wanting to represent Chrysalis in their particular country. Our bands were selling records everywhere, and at that time, we had no representations established. I remember two French publishers having a fistfight in front of me, both declaring they had been the first to contact me! I was literally working morning, noon and night – and I loved it.

I had to travel to each principle European country to choose representatives, and also to the USA. Chrysalis had a management base in New York, run by Terry's university friend, Derek Sutton. This was an impressive apartment on E65th Street, where Terry and Chris could base themselves when organising the lengthy US tours for Jethro and TYA. I got on great with Derek, and was invited to stay there whenever I was in New York.

However, I chose Los Angeles to be my HQ in terms of music publishing. LA in 1969 was a very different place than it is now. I think the city has been ruined by overpopulation. The exodus from other cities and states in the recent years has resulted in people recreating what they had been striving to get away from. In those days, to me, it felt more like Mexico! It was hot, beautiful weather, lots of Spanish spoken, no one seemed to be in any kind of rush. Freeways were empty and I rented my dream car at that time – a Ford Mustang Fastback. I was in heaven!

I chose Rondor Music, run by the legendary Chuck Kaye, to be our US representatives. They were the sister company of an impressive label called A&M Records, co-owned by former record promotion executive Jerry Moss, and the massively successful recording artist Herb Alpert. This was the beginning of a very longstanding, fruitful relationship, as some years later I went on to run their UK operation.

A friend at CBS Records in London, Dave Margereson, played me an advance copy of the first single to be released in the UK by a new American band called Santana. They first came to prominence after performing their song *Soul Sacrifice* at the Woodstock Festival in 1969. Their Latin-rock fusion led to a total of eight Grammy awards and numerous chart albums.

A friend played me the first single by a new American band called Santana

The track Dave played to me was called *Evil Ways*. I was instantly gripped by the guitarist's technique – lightning-fast runs played like needlepoint, and the Latin/rock fusion that was their sound. I also noticed that instead of printing the name of their music publisher on the label, there were the magic words 'copyright control', which usually indicated that no UK representation had yet been established.

I was almost delirious with excitement. After making a few calls I discovered the band were in Europe, and were playing the following day at a festival in Montreux, Switzerland. I knew the event promoters, so faster that a speeding bullet, I hopped on a plane and appeared backstage at the concert. I tracked down the manager, a guy named Stan Marcum, who like the band was also from San Francisco. I did conclude that a deal could be made to represent them in the UK, and managed to convince them I was their best option.

Ten days later, I was in San Francisco, visiting the Santana HQ. I had tracked down their lawyer, who was based in LA, and we flew up to San Francisco together. I remember having to stand at the check-in, holding up the LP sleeve, so the lawyer, Herb Cohen, could recognise me. He was very together – a breath of fresh air in that camp at the time!

We managed to conclude a contract for Chrysalis Music to exclusively represent Santana for the UK, licensed from their publishing company Petra Music. The word 'Petra' was Spanish for rock. Santana had not toured in the UK at this stage, which was quickly rectified some short time later. They took the country by storm, selling out theatres and dominating the charts.

My talent-spotting ability was about to move up a gear

My rivals started to check them out, but discovered they were way too late. The early bird gets the worm! It felt great to represent both music that I absolutely loved, as well as making a positive career move. And my talent-spotting ability was about to move up a gear.

Rock Solid

Six

It's All Hunky Dory

Classic hit *Space Oddity* was one of my all-time favourite records. So it was a 'no brainer' when production company Gem asked me if I'd be interested in meeting David Bowie. Apparently he was looking for a new music publisher.

David visited me in my office one morning a week or so later, accompanied by his wife Angie. He played me a new track called *Holy Holy* – which I thought was great – together with compositions from his then current album *The Man Who Sold The World* on Mercury Records. David, Angie and I really hit it off. I was determined to convince my bosses to come up with the contractual advance of £5,000. Of course, that sum is peanuts now, but it was a large amount at the time. When I think of the initial advance of £250,000 I had to pay to secure The Spice Girls contract many years later, it amuses me to reflect on the moves I made regarding the Bowie contract. I wanted the safeguard of a watertight contract as 'so much' money was involved!

I decided to use a New York law firm, Kurtz and Vassallo, to draft the document. Normand Kurtz was recognised as being the 'hottest' music lawyer at that time. His fees were probably almost as much as the advance, though I certainly didn't think about that then. It's only occurred to me now, some thirty-nine years later! Chris Wright had to sign the cheque the day Bowie completed the contract. I remember his being very nervous over the amount.

'Go for it Chris,' I tried to assure him. 'If I had that sort of money myself, I would make the deal.'

I wasn't prepared for what came later, as I was about to discover. David immediately commenced my indoctrination into his fascinating world. I was invited down to his flat in Beckenham. This was basically the ground floor of a massive old house called Haddon Hall, and decorated by David in his inimitable style. I became a regular visitor over the next few months. We spent many an evening listening to all the music that interested David at the time, such as The Velvet Underground and in particular, Iggy Pop And The Stooges. One evening he played me a song he had just written called *Oh You Pretty Things*. He told me it just sort of came to him, in the middle of the night, and he had to get to a piano and play straightaway for fear of forgetting it. I was tremendously excited over the song's commercial sound. I was convinced it would be a hit.

> He played me a song he had just written called *Oh You Pretty Things*

Kid Jensen was an important disc jockey – and just as importantly – a fan of David's. Many people will also remember him as a *Top Of The Pops* presenter. The two of us had taken David over to Luxembourg to promote *Holy Holy* as a single.

Bob Grace and David Bowie in Luxembourg 1971

As a follow-up, Kid asked me to interview David in the London studios of Radio Luxembourg with a prepared script. Essentially, they would then edit out my voice and have it replaced by Kid's. So shortly after I'd heard *Oh You Pretty Things*, I found myself in the studio doing the interview with David. It went well. As there was some studio time left over – and a piano conveniently placed in the studio – I suggested David record a simple demonstration track of the song. His bracelets clattered a bit on his wrists as he played, causing a rather effective percussive element. That just added to the warmth of the demo.

David had talked to me at length about the plans he had to embark on the path to 'super stardom'. We both realised it would take the kind of money we didn't have at that time. It would need an extensive photo session, for starters. David also wanted to hire an independent PR company to launch a new image to the press. He described the new image he wanted to create. It was essentially Ziggy – a totally different look to the Lauren Bacall style he was then displaying, that of long flowing hair, sometimes with dresses. I recall an evening spent with David and Angie at a venue he frequented in Kensington High Street called *Yours Or Mine*. It was a gay club in the basement of a restaurant called *The Sombrero*. People still reminisce about this place on the internet to this day. I had never been to a gay club before and I was more than a little concerned about being seen in such a venue! I needed some moral support. So I brought a mate who worked for me, called Gordon Sutherland. I was shocked to see quite a lot of media people that I knew, canoodling on the dance floor. I remember having a long conversation with a fascinating guy who was a friend of David's called Freddie, who wanted to be a singer. I asked what he was currently doing for a living, and he told me that he was a seamstress!

Anyway, back to David's new demo...I took it to MIDEM, the annual music industry convention held in Cannes. The title is short for *Marché International du Disque et de l'Edition Musicale*, and it's been running every year since 1967. Musicians, businesspeople and journalists descend on the event for talks, showcases and product. It was the most exotic setting for a conference I had ever seen. Located on the beach in the South of France, even in January it was such a different world from what we had left behind a few hours previously in wintry England. It is usually sunny there at that time. The main promenade *La Croisette* along the beach is adorned with palm trees, deck chairs, and outdoor cafes. There are marinas at either end of *La Croisette*, sporting multi-million pound yachts.

To describe further the sheer decadence of this setting, on a completely different occasion, when Rondor Music was placing the emphasis on international affairs, myself and the other directors of the company rented a huge yacht in the Old Port of Cannes at vast expense. The owner Captain Renault (yes, related to *the* Renault family) preferred the life of a sailor to that of the boardroom. We didn't actually sail anywhere, but we had daily receptions, parties and dinners for all of our foreign representatives to promote our company and clients. While nine of us slept on the boat, the accountants later discovered that most of us had also booked into hotels as well – 'just in case' a life on the ocean wave was not as idyllic as expected! Talking of sailors reminded me of a time when I returned from a trip to Switzerland on Bowie business, and I bought a white 'manbag' in a nautical style. I was carrying it the next time I met up with David, and he was so enthralled with this item that I couldn't wear it again in front of him again. Why I just didn't give it to him defeats me! Sorry, David.

The French love promenading, busily going nowhere, wandering slowly, with the ladies in mink coats, the men in cashmere, and the inevitable poodle at their side. You can even take dogs into restaurants at Cannes. I saw one Frenchwoman in a restaurant with her dogs seated next to her, being waited on. Chrysalis Music had a stand in the *Palais des Festivals*, the business centre. Our booth was decorated with photos and posters of our artists, and had the all-essential record player where I could play our new material to potential and existing clients. The UK's most successful record producer was Mickie Most, who had discovered and produced acts like The Animals, Herman's Hermits and Donovan – to name but a few. He was the undisputed king of the charts. Virtually everything he produced was a hit. His office – which he shared with Led Zeppelin's manager Peter Grant – sometimes resembled a doctor's waiting room, with a row of nervous song pluggers waiting to play their wares to Mickie. A man of few words, he would play the demos on

| He would play the
| demos on a beaten-up
| Dansette record
| player

a beaten-up *Dansette* record player. His reasoning? Well, if it sounded good on that, it would sound great on anything more sophisticated! His unerring ability to spot a hit meant if he didn't like a song within about thirty seconds, it was all over. Conversely, if he played it to the end it usually signified he was interested.

Not wanting to blow my reputation with Mickie, I was very cautious about selecting songs to play him. As a consequence, my visits were seldom. However, I was convinced Mickie would love *Oh You Pretty Things*. Knowing he always came to MIDEM, I determined to track him down. Unlike us mortals in grotty hotel rooms, Mickie had a villa in Cannes. I knew that ultimately, he would make a visit to the Palais. Towards the end of the conference, word was out that Mickie was approaching, and I dashed down to the street to accost him. Spotting him, I managed to convince him it was worth his while to come straight to my stand to hear this song. Nervously, I put on the track, hoping desperately he would like it. Mickie was somewhat expressionless when concentrating. It was hard to get any clues as to whether he liked it or not. A good sign was that he heard it to the end. An even better sign was when he looked at me, smiled, and simply said, 'Smash'. He explained he'd been looking for the right songs for Herman to launch his solo career. Herman's real name was Peter Noone, and Mickie decided on the spot this was the song to do it.

David was between record labels. So we decided to let Mickie have the song for Peter Noone, instead of David saving it for himself. I was actually delirious with excitement at the opportunity presented by Peter. It would be the first time I would've been directly responsible for having a hit record. Additionally, I promised David I would direct the proceeds into promoting his new image – instead of using them to recoup the advance. The single made top twelve in mid-1971, six months before David's debut album for RCA, *Hunky Dory*, was released. David played piano on Peter's record. We also secured the 'B' side with the song *Right On Mother*. With the proceeds from this hit in the pipeline, we went ahead with funding David's new image. I'd befriended photographer Brian Ward, who Terry Ellis had used for many of the classic Jethro Tull shots. I introduced him to David. A photo session was soon booked, resulting in the cover photo for *Hunky Dory* – along with the now classic shot of David in a phone booth on the cover of the *Ziggy Stardust* album. That phone booth was located right outside Brian's studio in London's Heddon Street. It's still there today, adjoining a wall with a plaque officially commemorating the event. Armed with a bundle of photos representing his new image, David, myself and newly appointed publicist Bill Harry, set off for Fleet Street to update the editors of the music press. Bill was the man of the moment as he was from Liverpool, and also a good friend of all the Beatles. He'd also been editor of the influential magazine *Mersey Beat*. First stop was an important magazine at that time called *Record Mirror*, which had always been well disposed to Bowie. Following a cue from him, I distracted the editor, Peter Jones. While we chatted, David went to the filing cabinets, withdrawing photos of his previous image, and replacing them with the new shots!

While this type of activity was an unusual business landscape for a music publisher, we were doing all these things together because David was concerned that his management company wasn't taking enough care of him (which proved untrue). But due to this insecurity, he latched onto me as his career lifeline at this time, which sometimes felt a little claustrophobic. I probably also had a degree of insecurity of recouping the 'vast advance of 5K' and making David a star was a sure fire remedy for that! So I did put my time, heart and soul in helping David realise his vision of world domination (I'm not kidding!). As a result, I did rather neglect my responsibility in keeping his management – and indeed also my bosses – up to date with all our exploits in a bit of a Lone Ranger fashion. That created some friction, as you can imagine. It's interesting to note that at the time of writing this (May 2012), Chris Wright sold Chrysalis Music to the BMG Group for £107 million. I don't know the pro rata percentage of earnings derived from Bowie songs. But assuming only five per cent, that's over a £5 million return on the investment – over and above enjoying the annual profit of the catalogue for 40 years! But that's the music business. It's feast or famine.

David's manager Tony Defries had started taking note of the new action surrounding his client. My boss Terry Ellis called me into his office shortly after *Oh You Pretty Things* had charted. Thinking I was at least going to get patted on the back – or even better, a raise – I entered the meeting cheerfully. As I went in, I noticed also present was the manager Tony – and that both he and Terry looked decidedly annoyed. That perplexed me somewhat. Terry had a copy of music industry magazine *Record Retailer* open at the chart page.

'What's this?!' he exploded, pointing to the Chrysalis Music credit on the Peter Noone single. 'You've ruined the image of our company by associating it with this pop music.'

I was absolutely flabbergasted. Everyone else had been thrilled with my achievement. Furthermore, it transpired Tony had the wrong idea that I was trying to steal his client for management, by showering so much attention on David. I managed to calm them both down. First, I assured Tony I considered I was merely doing my job of developing David's writing career, and that Terry was needlessly worrying. Tony also told me he was in the closing stages of signing David to a major record deal with RCA. My relationship with Tony improved and grew from that moment. I remember accompanying him to Glastonbury by train, with David and Dana Gillespie, when David performed at the fledgling festival. He went on stage at sunrise – to the bemused stares of a small crowd of hippies who were tucking into their macrobiotic breakfast! That was the first and last time I ever attended Glastonbury, although I did experience The Isle of Wight extravaganza. Tony shared David's vision of being a superstar, and his 'virtual' mentor, Colonel Tom Parker – Elvis' manager – was a powerful and positive influence on him. I credit Tony with making an enormous contribution to David's eventual success.

David himself was very intense to work with. He wanted my undivided attention most of the time. I don't think he ever considered it important that I had other clients. To his credit, David was always so supremely confident that he was going to be a massive star, he considered I was wasting my time working with anyone else! Maybe he had a point. Sometimes he'd wait for me after work in his beaten-up old Rover, and whisk me down to Beckenham to share his ongoing plans for world domination (which obviously came true). A slight hiccup to the 'plan' was when I took David to a BBC studio in the Haymarket, called the Paris, where he was booked to perform some live material. Halfway through the set, he lost his voice, and couldn't continue. I remember that he was virtually inconsolable afterwards in the nearby pub, The Captain's Cabin, thinking his career was wrecked. Well, far from it as it turned out!

I'd rented an apartment in a block at Marble Arch, called Park West. It was quite fancy and boasted uniformed porters. It was a very impressive block of flats, with a very imposing entrance, sweeping drive and fancy flowerbeds. You then entered a vast reception area with porter's desk. An atmosphere of affluence pervaded everything. It was in reality only an illusion, as the rent wasn't that expensive. The difficulty was in getting hold of a flat to rent in the first place, as they were in short supply. A director of Chrysalis had the flat before me, and had passed it on. I was on the top floor, with views of Hyde Park. I stayed there for about a year until my lease was terminated very suddenly when the management discovered I had a dog, a tiny Jack Russell terrier, called Rufus. That's a hanging crime in Park West.

One evening I went home to relax after an intense day. Much to my astonishment, there was David Bowie – sitting in my lounge waiting for me! He'd talked his way past the porters and convinced them to open my flat with their passkey. He was always brimming with new ideas to share with me, as he needed assistance in getting them off the ground. These resulted in side projects such as The Arnold Korns, a local group of kids from Dulwich College who played on the demo of *Moonage Daydream/Hang Onto Yourself* which I convinced B&C records to release in May 1971. There was also a singer called Freddie, who I had met at the Sombrero, who David wanted to launch as Rudi Valentino. But it never came to much, as David's career began to take off, and he was consumed with all the demands that entailed.

I remember distinctly one conversation with Bowie because it felt so bizarre. I'd informed him that I wouldn't be around for a couple of weeks, as I was going to Ibiza with my girlfriend, Sarah. He asked what I was going to do, so I said to relax and sunbathe.

'Sunbathe,' he retorted, 'what for?'

'To feel good,' I said, 'to get a tan.'

'Why would anyone want a tan?" he said, being genuinely perplexed as to why people didn't want to stay white. He told me he would actively avoid the sun in his quest to stay pale.

David had a great instinct for spotting other people on the brink of success. One of these people was an engineer named Ken Scott, who worked at a hot London recording studio called Trident. Ken would go on to produce Supertramp, who I also published, and many other big acts. David invited me to Ken's house to choose songs for *Hunky Dory* from the load of demos that David had been putting down, along with a few songs he hadn't written.

> **David invited me to Ken's house to choose songs for *Hunky Dory***

In retrospect, it was great to have been part of that selection team for the songs which featured on such a momentous, classic album. I was also privileged to have birthed the title. I had spent a weekend with my old drinking buddies in Esher at a pub called *The Bear*. The landlord was the archetypal English 'chap' who talked like the Billy Bunter character from Greyfriars School. Even though he ran the pub, he also drank beer for England, and would be constantly exclaiming everything was 'hunky dory'. For some reason I shared this with David, who always seemed to be interested in eccentric people. The next thing I knew,

> **It's very 'Bowie' to pick up on things people say**

he'd picked that phrase for the album title! It's very 'Bowie' to pick up on things people say. Someone once said David was like a bee that takes all the pollen out of a flower, and then moves on, without looking back. That observation really sums up my relationship with David.

Once *Ziggy Stardust* took off, I began to lose contact with Bowie. I recall ringing him shortly after he'd launched his new Ziggy image via a performance on BBC TV's late-night rock show, *The Old Grey Whistle Test*. I'd noticed that a string on his guitar had broken, and as a guitarist myself asked him which one.

'The G string, of course,' he replied. That was a typical Bowie response.

Some time later, David changed all his phone numbers and relocated. It was a relief in some ways, as I was able to focus on my other clients, without the intensity of David or Angie wanting something every five minutes. Of course, I still had the exclusive worldwide publishing rights to his songs for the duration of the contract – which proved to be 'watertight' – and the Chrysalis Group still owns the cream of Bowie songs today. The only sadness I felt was the loss of a friend. David had become a good mate, and I really enjoyed the stimulus of his company.

Years later, when he'd become the superstar he predicted, I was overjoyed to bump into him at a very fancy restaurant in Paris. In my experience, stars have one thing in common. They like to socialise with people who were friendly with them before they were famous, as they know the friendship was genuine. Accordingly, Bowie, being no different, dismissed the journalist with whom he'd been intending to have dinner, and suggested I dine with him instead. After my understanding dinner date also left, David and I had a great catch-up session, which was very cathartic. He apologised for 'dumping' me, but explained at the time, in a 'Greta Garbo' moment, he had cut all ties with his past. Whatever!

I recall he told me in detail of his drug usage, and how he had overcome it. I was very interested in his response, having to commit to a 12-Step programme myself to achieve sobriety. He said his usage was entwined with the 'Thin White Duke' persona that he had been flaunting. His remedy was to lock the image in a wardrobe in a hotel room in Los Angeles, and take the key with him on checkout. That's a new way of handling recovery!

I met up with David more recently at a music industry lunch. They were honouring him with a lifetime achievement award. We had another good catch-up, with the obligatory hug. He was happily married, mature and wearing a suit. *Aladdin Sane* had become establishment!

Seven

One More For The Road

t sounds morbid. But it was very commercial. The song *Bury Me Deep In The Ground* was recorded by a rock band from Barnsley, Yorkshire, fronted by a talented pair of songwriters named Paul Travis and Barry Lord. Shortly after Bowie had taken off, I was introduced to them, as they were represented by his management, Gem. They had a producer, also represented by Gem, Chris Demitrou, who was and is a great encourager. I proceeded to sign the band as songwriters to Chrysalis Music, hoping the record division would be interested as well.

Alas, like Bowie, whom the label turned down, I experienced the same negative reaction to this band, who went on to be named Sunrise. I became rather disenchanted with the Chrysalis management at that time, and started looking for pastures new. I'd received some interesting offers from rival organisations, notably from the management company of Graham Gouldman, one of my writers, who wanted to finance me as an independent music publisher. I didn't take them up on the offer, as I knew I didn't have enough experience at that time. But I was later encouraged by Graham's eventual success as founder member of the wonderful 10cc.

Chrysalis founders Terry Ellis and Chris Wright continued to maintain the management of their respective groups, Jethro Tull and Ten Years After. I started thinking that maybe artist management was the direction I should follow. My father was a successful manger, so perhaps it was my destiny. As they say, how dumb can you be and still breathe! I genuinely thought management would be easy. After all, Terry and Chris did it while building up a record company and agency at the same time. So it must be a piece of cake. It turned out to be a huge learning curve for me –by gaining experience of how not to do it. You name it, I did it wrong.

I left Chrysalis, and started operating from home. I'd secured a good deal for the band with A&M Records, the hottest label at that time. I financed the band and road crew not only to come down from Yorkshire to Surrey – where I had relocated – but also to pay for their accommodation and living expenses from A&M's advance. On meeting them at Weybridge railway station, I had a sense it was going horribly wrong. I could see Paul Travis, but where was Barry Lord, co-writer and singer?

''Appen he's left the group,' said Paul in his strong northern accent, 'but don't worry about it.'

'Worry' wasn't a strong enough word to sum up my feelings. Panic would have been more appropriate. Anyway, I soldiered on, organising rehearsals, buying equipment, and so on. I was feeling rather depressed, as it had dawned on me I wasn't cut out for

> **The lorry shook, the kiosk shook, I shook**

this particular lifestyle – and most certainly wasn't enjoying it. Take driving a truck, for example. I had to rent a truck to collect the new PA system, and drive it back to Surrey from North London. I got nearly all the way back and decided to pop into the pub for a 'quick one'. We all know that's a lie. A quick one led to a slow few. Coming out of the pub tanked up, I thought the truck should be tanked up too, so I went off for some petrol. I swung into the Esso filling station at Weybridge, forgetting I was in charge of a truck, and – with a mighty 'bang' – impaled the corner of the roof on the corner of the awning of the garage kiosk.

The lorry shook, the kiosk shook, I shook. The only person who didn't shake was the clerk inside the kiosk. He seemed oblivious to what had happened. Gingerly, I reversed, filled up with petrol, and with trepidation went into the kiosk to pay. It was then I realised the clerk was a teenager, so high on marijuana he hadn't the faintest idea the incident had happened! There was little or no damage to the garage, so I didn't bother to enlighten him. However, that wasn't so true for the truck, whose roof was ripped open like a sardine tin.

It would be true to say by this point, I'd become way too reliant upon alcohol and dope in a bid to relax and de-stress. Deep down, I was aware I'd bitten off more than I could chew with managing this group. I wasn't enjoying the experience at all, and was in some despair, as I couldn't see the way out. I knew the funds would eventually run out, and the fear of this would grip me from time to time. I was learning the hard way there is no money at all in the first few years of developing a group.

With the travel expenses, it actually cost more to play a show than we got paid. Staying in hotels after a gig was out due to the cost, so we'd often drive home in the early hours of the morning. For example, we had the opportunity of supporting Slade in Bournemouth for the princely fee of £25. It cost more on petrol alone to do that show. Often promoters wouldn't even pay you any money, despite the fee agreed in the contract. They often resembled retired boxers, and dared you to challenge them to pay up, surrounding you with a few equally mean-looking bouncers. I rapidly came to the conclusion this life wasn't for me. It was too rough. I longed for my old life as a creative consultant to artists within the context of music publishing.

I became so stressed, I realise now I was having a bit of a nervous breakdown. I was living a godless, hedonistic life, so in retrospect it was no wonder this was going on. I was at the end of my tether and did something quite radical for me at that time. I found a church one weekday morning that was open, sneaked in and found myself a pew in a secluded corner. I actually prayed for help... to a God I didn't believe in.

Looking back, I now believe God heard me and answered my prayer. But I didn't acknowledge that until years later. I remember hoping no one would see me coming out of the church afterwards. How crazy is that? I didn't mind people seeing me legless in a pub or at a party, but coming out of a church – that was a disgraceful act! As I only knew two modes of living – working hard or partying hard – I resolved to fix the situation by trying to get another job.

As is often the case, the best jobs never seem to be available when you need them. Initially, I couldn't find any openings. Beggars can't be choosers, so when an opportunity presented itself to work with a company – somewhat chaotically run to say the least – I had to take it. They offered to take on the responsibility of handling the management of Sunrise, while paying me a small salary to run their music publishing company. To say this was a relief is a massive understatement. This was a management company run by two lovely guys, Robert and Grenville.

They were what we called at the time, 'Hoorays', who had discovered The Kinks when they were playing at a party for the 'deb set'. I don't know how they had previously run their company, but I felt they were unaware of the responsibilities of launching a music publishing company.

Noticing I was extremely tense most of the time, they sent me off to Majorca – at my expense – for two weeks to stay at the 'Sea Club' in Cala Ratjada. The place was populated with all their hooray friends with whom I had nothing in common. More stress! On my return Robert, Grenville and partner Ray Williams were managing a band who were also with A&M Records called Stealer's Wheel, who went on to enjoy some notable success, and the office atmosphere grew more positive. There were often plenty of interesting people around, such as June Bolan, widow of Mark, and Frankie (a lady) who had formerly been PA to over-the-top 60s DJ Simon Dee. I'd also embarked on a relationship at this time with a Weybridge girl, Sarah Bodenham, which proved to become eventful.

I was at a very low ebb. Tearfully, I unloaded all my problems one morning onto my friend from Shepherd Market time, fellow music publisher Derek Green. Innocently, he'd enquired how I was doing! It just so happened that Derek's bosses at A&M Records in Los Angeles wanted to promote him from running their UK publishing company Rondor Music, to heading A&M Records UK. That was a big jump in expertise and responsibility. The only fly in the ointment was that Derek was reluctant to leave Rondor until a suitable replacement could be found to nurture the stable of writers he'd signed over the previous three years. I was the logical candidate.

I'd secured the job at Rondor for Derek in the first place, recommending him, after rejecting their earlier offer for me, as their first choice candidate to leave Chrysalis and establish a presence for Rondor in the UK. A&M bosses Herb Alpert and Jerry Moss had known me before Derek, as I had chosen them to represent Chrysalis Music in the USA, and presumably they were impressed with the job I did there. Anyway, to make a long story even longer, I became general manager of Rondor Music (London) Ltd in 1972.

The client list Derek had built up was impressive, and there were definitely big shoes to fill if I was going to make a success of this. My first task was to get to know all the staff, and to pretend I knew what I was doing. The second, and equally daunting, job was to get to know all the writers, their songs and managers. Some had become very successful, so this endeavour had its challenges. In no particular order, the UK clients were – Johnny Nash, Bob Marley and The Wailers, Yes, Rick Wakeman, Albert Hammond, The Doors and Richard Kerr. Additionally, the staff writers at head office in Los Angeles were very keen to meet me, as I would also be responsible for helping develop their careers. Some of them were very high profile professionals indeed, such as Paul Williams and The Carpenters.

In truth, I found the pressure overwhelming at times – particularly as I wasn't confident I had the necessary skill set to run such a big operation. I was 26, self taught in business, and saddled with a daily hangover, as I needed a good drink to overcome my doubts and fears. After the mess-up with Sunrise I felt this was my last chance, and was desperate to make it work. To compound the stress, I also had that nagging voice at the back of my head which constantly said, 'And which stars are you going to find and develop?'

The failure rate of new artists in the UK was about 95 per cent, and all my competitors were also looking for the next big thing. I put much time and energy into working with Richard Kerr and Albert Hammond. Richard had enjoyed a big hit a year earlier with a song called *Brandy*. Co-written and performed by Scott English, it was a top ten record. Later it was re-titled *Mandy* by Barry Manilow and became his first gold record and first US number one in 1974.

Albert had written and recorded many previous hits, including but not in anyway limited to *A Way Of Life* by Family Dogg in 1969, *Little Arrows* by Leapy Lee also in 1969, *Freedom Come Freedom Go* by The Fortunes in 1971, a number one in the USA for himself in 1972 with *It Never Rains In Southern California* – plus his own UK hit *Free Electric Band*, a top ten record in 1973. A big break came for Albert and me in 1974. The Hollies had a huge hit with a cover version of one of my all-time favourite Albert Hammond songs, *The Air That I Breathe*.

I thought my stress came from the pressures of business, not from underlying unresolved emotional problems, compounded by daily drinking. So I saw booze as the way out of this mess. This led to a series of poor decisions – ranging from drinking companions to a disastrous marriage. I was still going out with Sarah, who was very keen to wed. Being so insecure at that time, the notion of such a commitment terrified me. However, in a 'weak' moment we got engaged, and I endured – but never enjoyed – the celebrations and attention from her family. They were Roman Catholic, and insisted Sarah and I went to a church dignitary, called a 'monsignor', for religious instruction. He didn't like me on sight, and I must say the feeling was mutual. The upshot of all this was that I broke off the engagement, to the fury and embarrassment of Sarah's family. She was banned from contacting me for 'her own good'.

Some weeks later, in defiance of her parents' edict, we did see each other. In another not so brilliant decision I concluded the problem wasn't me, but was the pressure of a formal wedding. So we eloped, and got married with a few pals as witnesses a week later. We actually went on honeymoon to Dublin with friends. How odd is that! There was much drinking, so I suppose the home of *Guinness* was the ideal place. We went on from there to Malta, where my parents were living, to break the news to them, and have a quieter honeymoon in the sun. My mum took one look at my stressed-out condition and tossed me a book on yoga.

'You've made your bed hard, so lie on it,' were her immortal words to me.

I rented a furnished flat in Lower Sloane Street for a few months. Then I bought a house in Weybridge, near her parents, and tried to make a go of the relationship. My basic method of 'making the marriage work' was to keep topped up on alcohol, trying to balance having enough to take the edge off the stress, while being sober enough to function. It was an approach that was bound to fail. My work suffered, as I couldn't work creatively while being profoundly unhappy. The hangovers didn't help, either!

About 18 months later, in January 1975, I was in Cannes again for MIDEM, the annual International Music Industry Conference. I was confronted by my boss from the USA. He wasn't satisfied with my performance, to say the least. I knew I had what it took to be a success, and for the first time told him, an outsider, that I was in a very unhappy marriage, and that it was affecting my work adversely.

'Then shape up or ship out,' he told me, not too sympathetically. I went back to my room, and shared with a colleague what had just gone on.

'How do I leave home?' I mumbled. Then, in a 'eureka' moment, I had the answer. Packed with my favourite clothes, my case was on the other side of the room, and my passport was in my pocket.

'I've already left,' I reasoned with myself.

I'd thought of this moment dozens of times before. But I'd imagined doing it at home, with a frantic Sarah screaming at me as I emptied drawers. I decided then and there that I wouldn't return. I'd dedicate myself to getting my act together, and take care of business in a thorough way. I actually started enjoying MIDEM, from that moment on. Upon my return to England, I booked a room at my favourite hotel, Blakes, and made the call to Sarah. To be honest, she wasn't surprised, and was probably as relieved as I was, as she could see we were going nowhere fast together. My old friend Tim Knight kindly put me up at the flat in Shepherd's Market again, without charging me any rent. That enabled me to make a fresh start.

Through Tim, I met his buddy, Peter, who was a great guy. Peter, a former amateur boxing champion in the UK, had gone downhill after that achievement as a result of overdoing the alcohol, and happily sorted himself out by attending Alcoholics Anonymous meetings. I'm deliberately not mentioning his surname, as a condition of AA membership is maintaining anonymity. I obviously knew about drinking, and 'going on the wagon'. But I'd never considered the possibility of living without alcohol until I met Pete.

He was confident, happy, and able to socialise without the need for a drink. I wanted what he had. After a heavy night's drinking a few weeks later in Spain, where I was on holiday with Tim and Pete, he asked me if I'd had enough. I was relieved that Pete asked me. I couldn't stand the hangovers any more. He shared with me, as they say in AA, that you don't give up forever, but you do it daily. He said it was much easier to stick to something for 24 hours than make a lifetime commitment – and you have to attend AA meetings regularly.

Like all newcomers, I was encouraged to attend 90 meetings in the first 90 days if I was serious about staying sober, and start working through their 12-step recovery programme. I started immediately upon my return to the UK in June 1975.

Eight

Stone Cold Sober At Last

Living sober was wonderful. I felt liberated from 'the old life'. I was no longer hanging out in pubs and clubs – unless I had a real reason to be there. Working in the music industry as a talent scout, I had to go out a few nights every week to check out new bands, and keep in touch with existing clients.

It was the summer of 1975. I was still living at Tim's flat in Mayfair, which was great. I was working very hard at my job and at the AA recovery programme. I was able to be in work promptly in the mornings, which was a novelty. I noticed my staff were working harder as well, probably as I was setting a higher standard – at last. After work, I'd usually go to a meeting, have a bite afterwards with some of the AA members, and go on to a concert after that if necessary.

The basic concept of AA is to admit we are powerless over alcohol. The idea is to, stay away from the first drink a day at a time, and admit our lives are unmanageable unless we hand the running of our live to a 'power greater than ourselves'. AA encourages a broad understanding of what or who this higher power may be, so recovery is inclusive for everybody – regardless of their belief. Some members already had a traditional concept of God. Others used the power of the group.

> **The basic concept of AA is to admit we are powerless over alcohol**

Some used Good Orderly Direction as a 'God' concept. There were a hundred other variations.

One rather eccentric member, a recovered vagrant, would retreat into public phone booths, with no money, lift the receiver and talk to his 'higher power', who he called 'Paddy'! I wouldn't encourage this method as a norm, but it worked for him, as he kept sober and became well – physically, mentally and spiritually. As I was into yoga and meditation at that particular time, I was happy to trust God as my' higher power' in a cosmic kind of way. I walked and talked regularly with my invisible friend.

The common experience of most members was that quality of life steadily improved as we stayed away from that first drink, a day at a time, went to meetings regularly and worked the programme. As they used to regularly say about drink for the addicted, 'One's too many, a hundred's not enough'. I have to say the improved quality of life was definitely the case for me. I had a newfound peace of mind. I had reliable friends – not the 'fair weather' variety you meet at the pub – and new interests, by learning tennis. I was working hard – I got the thumbs-up from my employers, who liked the new me – and having hit records.

I signed the publishing rights to the songs of highly respected singer/songwriter Joan Armatrading. She started to become very successful in 1976, with her eponymous self-titled album and major hit single *Love And Affection*. There was a problem with a former publisher who we found out were still owed a few songs, even though the term of the contract had expired. The lawyers took a few years to sort things out, and *Love And Affection* had already been a hit. At stake were 21 songs, the copyright ownership to be decided by a toss of a coin, with *Love And Affection* being worth two songs. There was much tension in the room, but I won the toss resulting in only getting the alternate choice of ten songs, but including the all-important L&A.

I also heard some songs around that time by what I thought was just a new writer, named Rod Temperton. I remember thinking not only the songs, but also the production of the demos, were very strong. I'd initiated a policy at Rondor, that on Tuesdays I would see anyone personally and hear their demos. This was quite an unusual practice in the music industry at that time. Usually, songwriters had to be championed by an industry professional such as a lawyer or manager.

Rod had rung up for an appointment, saying he would only play his songs in person. Most companies would just say, 'post them in'. But Rod came in on the next available Tuesday, and I decided to give him a publishing deal on the strength of his songs. Even though Rod was a white boy from Grimsby, the songs had a black R'n'B feel, and I felt they would do well in the USA.

What Rod didn't tell me until after I promised him a deal, was that he was actually keyboard player in a band called Heatwave, who had just signed a record deal with a hot label called GTO. Label boss Dick Leahy told Rod not to tell publishers about the

Left to right: Kathy, Rod's Partner, Bob Grace, Rod Temperton

recording contract, as they would sign on the strength of the contract – not on the quality of the songs. No wonder the 'demos' sounded so slick! This was the beginning of an amazingly successful time for Rod and myself. The first single from Heatwave – *Boogie Nights* – went to number two in the chart the following year in the UK and USA, also followed by the hit album *Too Hot To Handle*.

About three years later, Rod decided to quit the band to concentrate on songwriting. We had a meeting to discuss the way forward. I talked it over with my colleague in the States, Chuck Kaye, who subsequently went to see Quincy Jones, with a copy of Heatwave's album under his arm. Quincy, or just 'Q' to his friends, absolutely loved Rod's work. He invited him to come over to the US and work on Michael Jackson's new solo album. Rod ended up writing the title track to the album, *Off The Wall*, as well as the classic *Rock With You* which became a number one single in the US in 1979. He also worked on the follow-up album, again writing the title track *Thriller*. That album went on to sell more than 100 million copies worldwide. The recording won eight Grammy's in 1984.

| **Rod ended up writing *Off The Wall* and *Thriller*** |

Rod also went on to write hits many other artists, including, but not limited to George Benson, Michael McDonald, and Anita Baker. You can't always believe the press, by the way. I remember being in the office with Rod when the first review of the *Thriller album* in the prestigious pop paper *Melody Maker* was brought in. A reviewer slagged off the album with the headline, *The Thrillhasgone*. Rod was – and still is – one of the nicest people you could meet, with outstanding generosity and integrity unseen in my experience in the music business. A few years ago, he hosted a 'thank you' party for everyone who had participated in his career over the previous 20 years. He flew about 50 people – including myself and my wife Yvonne – to an island in Fiji to celebrate, all at his expense.

The years 1975 and 1976 were proving to be vintage for hit writers at Rondor. Gallagher and Lyle had written a song called *Breakaway*. Graham Lyle was keen for me to try to organise a cover version. I represented the songs published by a top American record producer Richard Perry. It just so happened he was in London, putting the strings on a new solo album by Art Garfunkel. I put a call in to Richard to say 'hello'. He asked me if I had a song for Art, as they still hadn't found the elusive first single. We had a meeting the following day at Richard's suite at the Dorchester Hotel, with my talented Creative Director, Kevin Eade. On hearing *Breakaway*, Richard went absolutely bananas, and lo and behold, into the room walked Art, equally enamoured with the song. Apparently, he had been listening on the other side of the door!

Within ten days, the track was recorded and became the first single. It was a big hit on both sides of the Atlantic, and the title track of the album. After Gallagher and Lyle split up as a duo a few years later, Graham went on to specialise in writing songs for other artists. He enjoyed considerable success, writing major songs for Tina Turner, starting with *What's Love Got To Do With It* – co-written with Terry Britten – which was number one in the USA for three weeks, and *I Don't Wanna Lose You*, co-written with Albert Hammond.

My parent company A&M were enjoying much success with a rock group called The Police. Their manager invited the label to check out his new group Squeeze, at a club in Deptford one Tuesday. This was about two years after I'd gone sober, in 1977. The appointment clashed with another event, and in an attempt to comply with the request, the boss of A&M, my friend Derek, asked if I would go on their behalf. I dutifully set off to Deptford to the Albany Club as it was called. I was checking out bands regularly at that time, as 1977 turned out to be a vintage year for British rock bands.

I asked my AA friend Peter to come with me, so I had some sober company. As usual, the stage time was incorrect. I'd been told 8pm, but this turned out to be the stage time for the support group, and Squeeze wouldn't be on until 10pm. The manager had done a good job of getting the talent scouts out, but most of them adjourned to the pub until 10pm rather than bother with the support act. Clearly the pub was the last place I intended to go, so Pete and I stayed to watch the first act.

That turned out to be one of my better decisions, as the group was Dire Straits, who lived in a local flat by all accounts. I absolutely loved their set, recognising the brilliance of Mark Knopfler's playing and songwriting. This was only their tenth gig, since the former English teacher started the group, and the set was

> **I recognised the brilliance of Mark Knopfler's playing and songwriting**

basically the material from the first album. Squeeze were also great, and I had the high-class problem of deciding which band to pursue for exclusive representation.

Being somewhat daring – or impetuous – by nature, I ended up signing both bands to a worldwide contract. Squeeze was more straightforward as I was already friends with their manager Miles Copeland, but signing the Straits took a little longer – a year, in fact. Their lawyer, Robert Allan, who I knew well, had decided to hold off on making a publishing deal until the band had signed a recording contract. I had serious competition from Virgin Publishing – but common sense prevailed – and I eventually won the contract!

The Straits initially had success in Holland, playing to a festival of 100,000 one night, and playing to a half empty pub in Leicester, England, the following day! That was just a temporary blip, and the Straits shortly enjoyed huge international success, selling more than an astonishing 100 million records worldwide during their career. As my company had the exclusive right to collect all the songwriting royalties, their success also had a massive impact on the company I ran, Rondor Music, and me personally. This was all the more poignant as despite the band's wishes, and my persuasive powers, for whatever reason my parent company A&M couldn't see the potential in Dire Straits, and had turned them down. Well we all make mistakes. I was no different, having declined to try to sign both The Stranglers and U2 – who I

| We all make mistakes. I was no different, having declined U2

saw play in pub gigs – who I now love! I actually saw U2 in a small basement club called "The Rock Garden" in London's Covent Garden area. The cramped environment didn't really work for U2, in my mind, and I thought it was odd how singer Bono was marching around a tiny stage. No wonder they had to progress to stadiums! Well, if you're going to get in wrong, get it really wrong!

My bosses at Rondor promoted me to managing director of the UK company, and installed me in a newly created position as President of Rondor Music International. This effectively made me the head of Rondor Music worldwide, excluding the USA, which I regarded as a huge honour, and which would never have happened without finding sobriety. I was able to employ a fantastic financial controller, Tom Bradley, now Chairman of royalty collectors MCPS, to be my number two. He had the unusual combination of being both a chartered accountant and a former professional musician – with a great contact personality to boot. We became a strong team, travelling the world together and establishing the business.

By 1985, I started to become a bit restless, and was considering a new challenge. I had continued to find hits acts after Dire Straits, such as Nick Kershaw, Jim Diamond, Climie Fisher and a few others. Derek Green had decided to leave A&M and branch out with his own label. I was offered the opportunity of running A&M Records in the UK. I decided against this, and instead chose to join Derek in his new adventure, China Records and our new jointly owned publishing company, Empire Music.

I've never been exactly clear as to why I would leave a secure job, on a massive salary, to enter the insecure world of being an independent. I think it was a combination of being a bit bored with the safety and routine, coupled with being rather co-dependent on Derek and wanting the excitement of a new challenge. At any rate, January 1985 was the reality check as we started the launch of our new venture.

Nine

Something Inside
So Strong

Our debut act was a Yorkshire singer/songwriter with the slightly odd name of Kevin Kitchen. Everyone associated with us was very excited about this project, as Kevin had distinctive vocals and great songs. We were able to enlist the record production services of top producers Tony Swain and Steve Jolley – who'd enjoyed huge success with Bananarama and Alison Moyet. However, things didn't go exactly to plan.

The record took about nine months to make, and the 'sure fire' hit debut single entitled *Put My Arms Around You* didn't live up to expectations. With the benefit of hindsight, I think the timing was off. By the time the record was released, the public had moved on to a new 'sound' and the record was a bit dated. Also, Derek was, understandably, a little distracted by getting married and launching the Knebworth Festival all at the same time.

In Bible times, when people got married, the man took a year off work to spend time with his new wife. In fairness, Derek was aware at least of the demands of organising the show at Knebworth, which I supported. This was a massive undertaking, which was really a full-time job in itself. We also saw the power of musicians gathering for a cause.

The music industry's adopted charity was, and still is, Nordoff Robbins Music Therapy. This helps autistic, traumatised and mentally impaired children – and of course indirectly their parents – escape from the 'prison' of their condition through the power of music through trained therapists. The music industry, and virtually all major recording artists, wholeheartedly embrace and fund this wonderful organisation. Derek was a founder member of the fund-raising committee, with myself, and co-chairmen, Willie Robertson and Andrew Miller and others, when launched in the mid-70s. By 1986, the charity was in desperate need for a new centre to house the influx of music therapists needed to cope with the demands.

A few million pounds was needed to buy and fund this undertaking, and Derek felt very strongly it would have to be paid for in cash. The reason was that while the industry was happy to contribute to running costs throughout the year from fund-raising events, it wouldn't be so happy if the money raised were being used to pay bank interest and bankers' bonuses instead of directly assisting the children. So in the well-worn tradition of the music industry, the answer was to put on a show, inviting all the artists who had been the recipients of Nordoff Robbins Music Therapy awards at the preceding year's fund-raising events.

It took over three years to organise, mainly because of the complexity of rights issues over the live album. But it eventually took place on a rain-soaked day in June 1990, with headline acts such as Paul McCartney, Genesis, Dire Straits and Pink Floyd. All the financial goals were achieved. It may be a self-centred, brutal industry at times, but hearts seemed to melt where disadvantaged children were concerned. Major name artists were actually clamouring to be included in the show, for free. How rare is that!

A tense moment occurred when we heard Paul McCartney arriving

A funny, but tense moment occurred when we heard Paul McCartney's helicopter arriving. Paul and Linda were strict vegetarians. Even their road crew had to abstain from meat. However, the backstage area had been sponsored by McDonalds –

along with giant posters and hamburger stalls! Had anybody cleared this with the McCartney's? Probably not! Would they refuse to perform, or what? The diplomatic skills of Derek, Andrew and Willie were put to the test. Mercifully, common sense prevailed – the show must go on, etc.

Back at the ranch, as they say, China and Empire had started to flourish. In the second year of business, the hits started to come. On the Empire side, I signed a group from Sheffield called *Living In A Box* and got them a deal with Chrysalis Records. Their debut single – also called *Living In A Box* – made top five in the charts. I'd also secured UK rights to the songs and songwriting talents of Albert Hammond, who I'd represented some years previously. He had written major songs such as The Hollies' hit *The Air That I Breathe*, Leo Sayer's smash *When I Need You* and *To All The Girls I Loved Before*, a hit for Julio Iglesias and Willie Nelson.

Bob Grace and Albert Hammond
© *Sylvan Mason Photographs*

Jefferson Airship had also recorded one of Albert's songs called *Nothin's Gonna Stop Us Now*. It was the theme song for a movie which flopped called *Mannequin*, but was so commercial that it went to number one in the UK hit parade.

On the China and Empire side, Labi Siffre was signed on the strength of a brilliant song called *Something Inside So Strong*. He'd seen a TV film from South Africa showing a white soldier shooting at black children, and that inspired him to write this song. Labi approached Derek, who he had worked with successfully in the past, with a

> **Labi Siffre was signed on the strength of a brilliant song**

'problem'. The song, which powerfully depicted overcoming apartheid, was under request for recording with former Eurovision winners Bucks Fizz. While flattered that someone commercially viable should want to cover one of his songs, Labi felt strongly that Bucks Fizz didn't have the *gravitas* required. Another artist, a famous female black singer, thought the song was 'too black' and wanted Labi to lighten the lyrical content for her. Derek's discernment was on the money. He told Labi he should record the song himself without changing a word.

Derek played the song to veteran record producer Glyn Johns, who'd worked with The Who, The Stones and The Eagles among others. He loved the song and 'got' how it should be recorded – with taste and integrity. I had fun tracking down a gospel choir to sing on the track, which was recorded on a shoestring budget.

> **Sales rocketed after *Wogan* – and radio came fully on board**

The record was released in 1987. Despite being well received by radio, it got off to a slow start, with a 'B' list rotation on Radio 1 – giving it about eight plays a week. 'A' is at least double that.

The situation dramatically changed when Labi was invited to perform the song live on the TV show *Wogan*. The producer had seen Labi perform on the lunchtime TV show *Pebble Mill At One*.

Sales rocketed after Wogan – and radio came fully on board. The record went to number four, giving China/Empire credits with three records in the top five simultaneously – Jefferson Airship at number one, Labi at four, and Living In A Box at five. Labi later received the music industry's most prestigious honour, the Ivor Novello Awards best song of the year, 1987.

Labi's composition was often used in Amnesty International campaigns. It became the title track of Kenny Roger's album in 1989. Living In A Box went on to enjoy commercial success worldwide. I managed to hook up Albert Hammond to write with them, resulting in two hits – *Blow The House Down* and *Room In Your Heart* – which went on to receive a gold disc for sales in excess of 400,000.

On the surface, all seemed well. I was still clean and sober. The new companies were doing well. The next band that Derek introduced to the company for recording and publishing rights, The Levellers, were to go on to be a major act, giving the company stability and a glowing reputation. However, I had the gnawing feeling in my stomach that something vital was still missing in my life. But I just couldn't put my finger on it.

> **I had the gnawing feeling that something vital was still missing**

The usual fix for this was to try to improve my love life, but this was proving problematic, as I didn't know where to go to meet girls.

The music business was not an ideal scenario for this, as most girls in the industry liked drinking/nightclubs and so on, and it was frowned upon to date in AA. Even though I had 'stuff' such as a nice house virtually paid for in Chelsea, a new BMW and a growing business, it wasn't 'fixing' whatever was ailing me. As a result I felt rather **R**estless, **I**rritable and **D**iscontent. As they said in AA, I had to get rid of RID. But how?

Rock Solid

Ten

Get Ready For The Grand Arrival

'd had a few encounters with 'churchy' people in the past. So I was wary of them. When I was growing up in Surrey, among our neighbours were some elders from a local church. Appropriately, their name was Abbot. They were, at least in my experience, very unfriendly, and never entered into the social activities in our road. We also lived next door to a vicar, and he never spoke to our family either – let alone share his faith with us. I later found out my dad had scared him off when he'd tried to evangelise!

However, I did attend another church, the Congregational, with my friend Peter Smithers, who lived in the same road. This was largely because of the youth group, YPF (Young People's Fellowship) that met every Friday night in the church hall. It was a good place to have fun. This also required church attendance, and because I was a good singer I was also in the choir. I must have had some religious instruction too, as I remember learning Bible verses up in my tree house before some test at church.

I don't ever remember being told the story of Jesus coming to earth and dying for me. But at least I attended for a while. This was at odds with my parents, particularly with my mother, who couldn't understand why I bothered to be involved at all. She told me it would be better if I had an open mind. In other words, drop it!

I did eventually drop attendance when I became a teenager, which is a common thing.

Shortly before I decided to quit drinking in 1975, I'd become fascinated with eastern mysticism and started checking out various meditation groups. I don't recommend meditation with a crippling hangover – you just get more in touch with how lousy you feel. In any event, I got involved in this area, running a mediation group in London, doing yoga, and even becoming vegetarian for a while.

I got involved in running a mediation group, doing yoga, and even becoming vegetarian

A&M Records had signed a brilliant guitarist called Bryn Haworth. They had engaged American record producer Audie Ashworth – famous for his work with highly regarded American guitarist named J J Cale – to make an album with Bryn. Even Eric Clapton was in awe of JJ's work, covering his songs *After Midnight* and *Cocaine*. The problem A&M perceived to have, was that in the interim, Bryn had found God, and was writing songs that didn't make sense to the label. The boss Derek Green rang me and asked me to go and see Bryn. Derek's reasoning was that as I was also 'cosmic', I could sort out Bryn and his songs. No problem, I thought. So one weekday morning, I travelled to his

A&M Records had signed a brilliant guitarist called Bryn Haworth

terraced house in Teddington, duly on my mission to 'sort him out'.

His wife Sally, was around, reading the Bible, and praying under her breath. Bryn turned my mission upside down by starting to sort me out instead, and telling me about Jesus! He talked about a broad way and a narrow way, and questioned which way was I on. I didn't really understand too much at that time, but realised that Bryn and Sally's utter belief in Jesus was not going to be undone by me or anyone else for that matter. I liked and respected them both enormously.

Saying 'goodbye' outside was interrupted by Concorde flying over. They were so near the airport, that the deafening plane actually darkened the street as its wingspan temporarily blocked out the sun. The buildings seem to shake with the vibration. Yet Bryn and Sally – clearly so used to this daily occurrence – didn't bat an eyelid! They just stopped talking in mid sentence, and continued where they left off after it passed, without even a comment.

I started playing Bryn's demos of his songs at home. They formed the basis of the album, which still came to pass called *Grand Arrival*. I was so taken with Bryn's music, and our encounter, that I got copies of the album's artwork from A&M's art department, and put them up on my wall at home. I still didn't really understand the significance of Bryn's lyrics, which were all about Jesus. But I knew they meant something important. I even started attending the church at the end of my street at Parson's Green in 1975 for about three months, but somehow I didn't 'get it'. A few years later I even went up to Holy Trinity Brompton in Knightsbridge, when they were holding what was called a 'Just Looking' evening for spiritual seekers. I quite liked the people, but was offended when they discounted my theories on reincarnation! I was put off for a while, well, seven years to be precise. They gave up on me. But God didn't.

In the late summer of 1988, there was a knock on my door in Chelsea. The wife of a friend of mine, Heather, who I hadn't seen around for a few months, invited herself in. She explained she had been back to her homeland of South Africa for the summer, had been taken to church, and had experienced an encounter with Jesus, which had captivated her. Probably remembering my previous attempts to know God, she wanted not only to share this encounter with me, but also to invite me to attend some sort of church group with her. So the next week, I drove out of central London with her, to a suburb called Raynes Park, and arrived at another terraced house.

Crammed into it were about 30 very enthusiastic Christians, playing simple worship songs on ropey guitars, praying and studying the Bible. It was a fledgling group led by John Mumford. I felt very uncomfortable and wanted to get out fast, but I was stuck. Later, I thanked Heather but explained it wasn't for me, and mumbled something about being too far away for me to attend regularly, all the traffic, and so on and so on etc.

However, all this got me thinking, as they say. Holy Trinity Brompton came back to mind. Their reputation locally was awash with reports of packed attendance on Sunday evenings, but with young people. In my limited experience, churchgoers were positively ancient by comparison. So I decided to attend the next Sunday. I knew the service started at 6.30pm, so I figured if I arrived at 6.29 no one would have time to 'bother' me. As it was, I got one of the last seats available, on a chair in the aisle at the back. Perfect.

There must have been a couple of hundred people there, predominantly in their early 20s, and looking quite good together. The worship band was pretty good, but it was hard to sing along, as I was totally unfamiliar with the material. The vicar, Sandy Millar, was absolutely riveting. His conviction and experience that Jesus was alive, active and well was contagious. He was a great raconteur, and communicated ably with us all. I managed to slip out unnoticed at the end, and went off by myself for a burger. I remember acknowledging it had been a powerful, memorable event, but reasoned it wasn't for me, and vowed never to return. After all, how would I be able to explain to my friends at work that I went to church? Embarrassing or what!

But the 'God thoughts' continued.

By the following Tuesday, all I could think about was that service. I started longing for Sunday so I could return. Within a month I was going not only in the evening, but also in the morning. Sandy Millar was challenging all my beliefs, and I was beginning to question my motives, morals and desires daily. Each week, he would cover a different area of failing in our lives that we should sort out. These are what the Bible calls 'sin'. If you felt this applied to yourself, you were invited to stand up, allowing those around you to pray for you. I was longing for a week when I had no need to stand! Try 'no sex outside the confines of marriage', for starters! One Sunday the then curate Nicky Gumbel announced the start of their 12-week enquiry course for people like me, called *Alpha*. Being curious, and a bit of a joiner, I decided to attend the following week.

I still felt very much an outsider, and was genuinely puzzled at the central Christian belief that Jesus was the only way to God. What about all the other religions? My concept of reaching God was quite different. Imagine a mountain, with God at the very top. There were many paths and approaches to the summit, and each religion had different ways to climb up. With that reasoning, it didn't matter which religion you belonged to, as it was the

> **It didn't matter which religion you belonged to, as it was the same God**

same God we were all trying to reach. That was my idea, anyway.

However, I turned up at the course each week in the church basement under the altar, called 'The Spring'. There was coffee, followed by a talk, and then we were separated into small groups of about 12. There were about 70 people on *Alpha* at that time. My small group was led each week by a very sweet guy named Nicky Lee. They seemed to be all 'Nickys' at HTB! We would discuss the talk, and air our feelings about the topic. At the end, Nicky would give us all a Bible verse to memorise during the week, and we would be 'tested' the next time. I was still rather rebellious, and dismissed the notion of complying with this request. However, I started thawing a bit, partly due to the embarrassment of never knowing the verse, and partly due to my growing high regard for Nicky, who seemed a good man.

I was still very hung up on Christianity being the only way. I hadn't a clue about salvation or how vital it was to receive it. I determined to read the verse of the week from the book of Revelation in that second volume of the Bible called the New Testament. The quote said, *'Here I am! I stand at the door and knock. If anyone hears my voice, and opens the door, I will come in and eat with him, and he with me'*. I used to say this prayer, out loud, on my knees next to my bed, before actually going to bed. The last night before the next Alpha meeting, I forgot, but remembered just as I was going to sleep. Reluctantly, remembering my vow to memorise this verse, I got out of bed and onto my knees – but with a cynical disbelieving attitude. This is literally how I said the prayer:

'Allo God, if you're there. Your word says, "Behold, I stand at the door and knock". They say that the door has no handle on the inside, because Jesus won't open the door and come in uninvited, and that it's up to me on the outside to turn the handle, and ask him in. So I say, come in, if you're there.'

I actually knocked on the wall, as if it were a door. But I didn't get much further. In that instance, an unseen power flowed all around me in that room, and a strange presence hit me like a tsunami. Wave after wave of bliss kept rolling over me, and I seemed to be thrown back to the other side of the room. It was almost unbearable but wonderful. After what seemed like hours, I actually asked it to stop so I could get some sleep. Meditation never had that kind of effect on me! I remember reflecting on the words from the co-founder of AA, Bill W when he had a 'mountain top' encounter with God – 'so this is the God of the preachers' – little believing that I too, would have a similar experience. But that's just what happened to me.

A strange presence hit me like a tsunami

God hit me like a freight train.

When I woke up the next day, the world wasn't much different from before. Things around me were still normal. But something else had changed. The Bible came alive when I read it. I knew God was real, that Jesus was alive and knew me and loved me. I realised the 'bliss' I had been seeking through drink and drugs was actually a desire to experience and know God in a real way. I discovered that Jesus calls it the *'peace that passes all understanding'*, and it was free for the asking. I remembered all the striving for that experience from doing hours of meditation and drinking – all to get a fake copy of the real thing. Later that night, everyone could see the difference in me.

All doubt in the existence of a God who loved me – and showed me that love – had been removed in a stroke. Nicky Gumbel asked me to share my story at the end of the *Alpha* supper. Participants invite friends and relatives to the dinner, to hear about what has been happening to them on the course, and to share an invitation to the next course.

It felt like God's DNA was now part of me. His values were becoming my values. Swearing and immorality no longer held any appeal. The Bible was now impacting me greatly, including such key sections as the Book of Romans. I realised that was telling me not to copy the behaviour and customs of this world, but to let God *'transform you into a new person'*. As I did that, the Book of Corinthians was coming true for me, where it says we're not the same anymore, *'for the old life is gone and a new life has begun'*.

Such a simple prayer had led to such a dramatic transformation inside me. I'd now chosen how I wanted to spend the rest of my life – and eternity – following Jesus. I found out a helpful description of a function of the Bible – 'Basic Instructions Before Leaving Earth'. I decided I wanted to dedicate the rest of my life to working out those instructions, through good days and bad.

Rock Solid

Eleven

Peace Train

I was getting stuck in at Holy Trinity Brompton. I was, consuming endless books on Christianity. And I was still attending AA meetings. After an AA meeting at a church in Knightsbridge one Monday evening, I joined the group for coffee and cakes afterwards. In walked this gorgeous, black American lady named Yvonne. In AA, it is common for people to be given nicknames to define them. For example, I was 'Bob the music', for obvious reasons, another Bob was 'Bob the hair', as he was a hairdresser. Yvonne's nickname was 'Beautiful Yvonne', very aptly named.

In walked this gorgeous, black American lady named Yvonne

I'd actually known Yvonne for a couple of years by then, though we weren't friends. In fact, we didn't like each other too much, as I remember. I thought she was rather standoffish, and apparently she thought I was a bit of a ladies' man. Anyway, we started talking that evening. It transpired that Yvonne had just returned from a tennis holiday in Portugal. Being quite into tennis at that time, I challenged her to a game, which to my surprise, she accepted.

We went out that evening for pancakes, with her friend Agatha. Unknown to me, Agatha had designs on me, but I had other ideas! Yvonne and I met at my house the following Saturday morning for coffee before the game. I showed her a photo album depicting the sad tale of the house burning to the ground two years previously, thinking this would elicit a bit of sympathy. In fact she thought this was a slightly odd gesture. Oh well, I tried!

We had a meal together at a local brasserie after the game, and got on really well. Yvonne decided I wasn't as superficial as she previously thought, and I also made her laugh a lot. That's always good therapy. What we really had in common was that we were both Christians, and we started going out together from that moment on. Naturally, I wanted her to come along to Holy Trinity Brompton with me, and fully participate there.

However, Yvonne was a member of a church in Marble Arch, and was singing in their choir. So we went along to each other's churches for a while, but couldn't agree on which one to join together. I suggested we draw up a short list of three different lively churches, and we could check them out together. Yvonne agreed, and we put a well-known church, St Barnabas in Kensington, at the top of the list.

I was driving by the following Saturday, and noticed it was open as a wedding was going on. I pulled into a parking bay, and popped into the church to have a peep. In the large lobby area were details of all their activities, courses and photos of the leaders. It looked very promising, and I slipped out without disturbing the wedding. Yvonne and I went along the following Sunday morning, knowing only that the vicar's name was John. We were shown to our seats, and informed that John was speaking that day.

John was hysterically funny, though slightly odd. But he was rather good. We found out later he was a visiting evangelist named J John – well known in church circles for his humorous stories – and not the actual vicar, John Irvine. Yvonne and I did Alpha again, this time together, under the leadership of Mike and Linda Clarkson, the American curate and his wife at St Barnabas.

Shortly after this, my niece Sophia got married to her man, Andy Crawford. It was a lovely spring day, and the wedding took place at Morden registry office, which is located in beautiful grounds.

I started thinking Yvonne and I should be next in line to be married. I approached John Irvine shortly after this, to get his advice.

'No problem,' he said, 'we'll just go over the "five C's".'

'The what?' I said.

'Just answer the next five questions, in turn, all beginning with C, and you can proceed – providing I give you a green light depending on your response. If you get a red light, we won't proceed any further. Is she a Christian?'

'Well, yes,' I replied.

'That's good,' I was told, 'because as a believer, God's Word says we should not be bound together with unbelievers.' That was the first green light!

'Now for "character". Is she a good, honest, truthful, reliable person etc?' John asked.

'Ugh. Yes,' I responded. That was the next green light.

'What about "chemistry"? Does she attract you physically? Does she turn you on?'

'Well yes,' I replied, 'obviously or I wouldn't want to marry her.' John then explained a number of would-be spouses, who wanted to experience marriage for whatever reason, fell at this hurdle because they were only friends with their partner, and somehow believed physical attraction would come later. John thought this was unrealistic, as usually, the burning passion experienced at the beginning of the relationship wanes rather than intensifies.

'Now for "circumstances". Is there a massive age gap or some other major obstacle that would make marriage unrealistic?' he said. I asked John for his advice on a mixed marriage.

'Absolutely no problem,' he responded. 'God looks at the heart, not your colour.'

'How about "counsel"? What do your friends and family think about your marriage plans?' This didn't mean we have to please everyone, but take heed if there's a wide raft of opinion advising against this step. As my friends and family loved Yvonne, and likewise with her friends and family, I got the final 'green light' in John's test.

'Oh whoops,' I said, 'does this mean I'm good to go and get engaged?'

'Absolutely,' was his prompt answer. But his advice was to make the engagement on the short side – a few months at the most – as it can be a busy, tense time, with many things to do and organise, let alone the rounds of relatives.

So with fear and trepidation, I got down on one knee a few days later, and stood up with a fiancée two minutes later! Yvonne and I were then invited by John to attend marriage counselling with him, both together and separately. I guess he had to ask Yvonne the 'five C's' on her own! It was absolutely wonderful and a privilege to have such quality, individual marriage counselling from such a wise and loving man as John, himself a family man. There was one little problem I had to deal with. That was fear of commitment. This manifested itself to me as a 24/7 panic attack.

There was one little problem – fear of commitment

It would abate at times, and intensify at others, but it wouldn't ever go away completely. This was one reason why I used to drink so much, in an effort to blot it out, I suppose. I'd experienced this before when I was first married, and it was a daily problem, which was always with me. I'd been engaged a couple of times afterwards as well, and the exact same thing happened, resulting in broken engagements, hearts, and distress all round.

Prior to meeting Yvonne, I was beginning to think I'd have to stay single the rest of my life – not because I would like that, but to avoid hurting other people again. I'd tried all sorts of remedies from shrinks, to self-help books and groups, but all to no avail. Now I was engaged to Yvonne, the fear returned, and I was beginning to panic.

I prayed. I mean, I really prayed. But I didn't talk about it, especially to Yvonne. About a week or so later, a packet arrived for me from my future mother-in-law, Mary, in New York, USA. It contained a small booklet, written by a well-known TV evangelist Kenneth Copeland, entitled *Freedom From Fear*. I was amazed, as Mary had no idea what I was going through. Even Yvonne didn't know, as I didn't want to alarm her. I discovered in reading the booklet that fear is an evil weapon launched against all people, and my only option to repel this force was faith.

'Fear is totally destructive,' said Copeland. 'It will cripple the mind, stop the heart, and even change the colour of your hair. Fear is a satanic force that works against you at every opportunity. Faith is a creative force that God uses to build and uplift. Faith helps; fear hurts.'

I looked up the most relevant scripture verses on fear and God's answer to that problem, and memorised them. I used about half a dozen. I realised that humanity's spiritual enemy – who the Bible calls 'Satan' – attacks all our senses. So I had to counter-attack by speaking out words from the Bible. The scriptures I learned at that time are now virtually tattooed in my mind! I typed out my half a dozen Bible verses, such as a well-known quote from the Book of Psalms – *'The Lord is on my side; I will not fear'*.

I put them all on the same piece of paper, and reduced it on the photocopier at work, so all the Bible references were on a tiny strip of paper, rather like a bus ticket. I folded it and kept it in my wallet. At every opportunity – from first thing in the morning to last thing at night – I'd get out this paper, hold it firmly in my hand, read it out loud and look at it. The grip of fear gradually became looser, even disappearing completely from time to time. Sometimes the fear would return, almost physically, like an avalanche, and I'd have to stop whatever I was doing, go somewhere I could go through the whole routine, and the fear would depart.

I remember being in the cinema with Yvonne, about halfway into our engagement, and suddenly I got this massive panic attack. I started reciting Bible verses like a weapon in my mind, but nothing happened. I excused myself, and went to the loo, which was mercifully empty. I got out my piece of paper, made my declaration, and the panic attack subsided.

I was hit by an absolutely massive panic attack about 4am on the first night of our honeymoon in St Lucia. I got out of bed, got my piece of paper, and literally wrestled with that fear for an hour-and-a-half until it fled, and I was consumed with wonderful peace.

> **I was hit by an absolutely massive panic attack about 4am**

I still carried my piece of paper everywhere, even though the attacks had abated a lot. I even put it in a waterproof bag inside my swimming trunks pocket. I had a panic attack walking on the beach, popped behind a sand dune and whipped out my Bible verses. Satan gave up after that! I found out the Bible assures us if we submit to God and resist Satan, he will flee from us, and God will come near. That's exactly what happened to me, as I recovered from my fears.

We were married on November 10th 1990 at a registry office in Hammersmith, followed by a blessing at St Barnabas conducted by John Irvine and attended by many friends and family. John told many humorous anecdotes relating to our lives. I remember my music business friends being astounded

> **We were married on November 10th 1990 at a registry office in Hammersmith**

that the vicar actually knew us. I was equally astounded by actually getting them into a church – under any circumstances!

The reception was pretty chaotic as we had to cram 80 people into a room with a capacity of about 50. The best man had to repeat his speech so people in the overflow room could hear it. Having said that, it was great fun, and a wonderful opportunity to share the story of Jesus with a captive audience. After a night at a luxury hotel in London's Mayfair, we jetted off to St Lucia in the Caribbean, followed by a second week in Grenada, two of the most romantic locations in the world.

Twelve

Stand By Me

From the Caribbean to cloudy London, a new adventure opened up for us. The house was very crowded as we basically had two of everything – sofas, toasters, kettles, tables and so on – and two of us! I carried Yvonne upstairs to her new home in the time-honoured tradition of newly weds.

She got to work very quickly in feminising the house. Impossible as it may sound, I had been able to exist without any cushions, any lace or frills or dainty artefacts. It would be safe to say I encountered a makeover. Yvonne has great taste and style, and an enormous capacity for 'getting the job done'. So it didn't take long for the transformation from my minimalist bachelor pad into our designer family home – packed with colour, flowers, photos and cushions everywhere!

Yvonne is a qualified Montessori teacher. Soon she found a job as a teaching assistant at a nearby primary school. The difference in our work schedules created a bit of conflict that had to be resolved. Yvonne had to be at work by about 8am whereas I didn't start until the crack of 10 (ish). However, I never knew when my workday would end, as 10am in Los Angeles, is 6pm in the UK, and I usually had a barrage of calls to make and receive.

Yvonne had also brought someone special to the house. That was her nine-year-old son Adrian, from her previous marriage to a senior executive in the cosmetic industry, who Yvonne had met while modelling in New York. I'd met Yvonne shortly after her marriage dissolved, and got on well immediately with Adrian.

Some doom-and-gloom merchants advised me against becoming a stepparent, with possible attendant problems. But apart from a couple of minor, normal adolescent incidents, I've never had a problem with Adrian. While always encouraging him to maintain healthy links with his natural father, who lived in New York, I've actively accepted the parenting responsibility. Adrian is now 31, lives in Bristol, and is an online marketing executive with a hot dot com company.

A year short of a day after we were married, Yvonne gave birth to a gorgeous little boy. We named him James – my grandfather's name as well as my and my father's second name. We gave him the second name of Christian for obvious reasons. Yvonne always says you couldn't ask for a better first wedding anniversary present.

However this 'gift' didn't come without its challenges. From an early age James often had problems with authority figures and settling in school in particular. The plans for his education didn't unfold in the way we had expected. We had to learn parenting skills in a hurry, and got enormous encouragement and help from Jim Fay's Love and Logic Institute in the USA. This was also a time when Yvonne and I had opportunity to express our faith on a regular basis!

James eventually secured some credible qualifications from a local college. He went on from there to the Philippines, where he volunteered to help with construction of a building project for a church that we had fund raised for a year earlier. He has recently returned to the UK where he is very happily employed in the catering industry.

Two years later in 1993, some more big changes started happening. I was offered a great job of establishing the UK office of a successful Japanese-funded American music publishing company called Windswept Pacific Music based in LA. I knew most of the major players in Windswept, as they were in senior management with Rondor Music some years previously. They had great faith in me. In the way typical to the LA music industry, I was pretty much given total autonomy to set things up, hire staff and get some writers. Much as I'd loved working with Derek, I felt my strength was better served in working with an established international team as opposed to going it alone as an independent company. I was able to bring our music publishing company, Empire, under the umbrella of Windswept for the UK. So I had the dual benefit of continuing my working relationship uninterrupted with my songwriters, along with accepting a new challenge that also brought job security. That's important to a married man with a young child. Plus, to be honest, I really wanted a change.

I found some great offices in a trendy part of Notting Hill Gate, and brought in Iqbal, the copyright and royalties consultant for Empire Music to not only do the same for Windswept, but also take on the responsibility for business administration. We got some great office furniture from Ikea, and I became quite skilled in flatpack assembly. We managed to rent an office, furnish it and sort out all the IT for less than the interior designer's fee for a rival organisation that was also setting up! The Pet Shop Boys' office were our neighbours – along with a few other music-related companies. So it was quite a stimulating, 'vibey' atmosphere.

> **The Pet Shop Boys were our neighbours – along with other music-related companies**

Iqbal and I decided to re-register all the songs in the catalogue, which numbered about 50,000 at that time. This painstaking job had the effect of massively increasing our income, as we were able to focus our undivided attention to detail on this crucial task. Windswept had established itself in the USA by getting huge funding from a Japanese corporation – 50 million dollars, to be exact. The initial leaders were music publishing veteran Chuck Kaye, former President of Rondor Music USA and later Warner Brothers Music and his stepbrother, music supervisor and soundtrack compiler, Joel Sill.

The plan, which turned out to be very successful, was to bring in a partner to finance the operation, buy established catalogues of older well known songs from the 50s, 60s and 70s, and place them in films to enjoy the lucrative money derived from soundtrack albums. They initially bought the music publishing from the notorious godfather of pop, Morris Levy, as it was the sister company of his label Roulette Records.

This $12 million deal was conducted in 1990, with the able assistance of lawyer Evan Medow, who would in later years become CEO of Windswept. None of the major publishing companies could deal with Morris as he was on bail following an appeal against his ten-year jail sentence for extortion, but that didn't deter the Windswept guys. The catalogue contained some wonderful classic pop songs from the 60s by Tommy James and the Shondells, such as *Mony Mony*, and Tiffany's *I Think We're Alone Now*. Chuck told me that Morris was so fed up with people pulling out of the deal – six in a row – for fear of dealing with a convicted gangster, that Chuck would have to pay $50,000 upfront just to discuss the deal, only to be repaid if completed. Chuck, a ballsy guy anyway,

Left to right: Bob Grace, Evan Medow, Sheryl Medow, Ichi Atsatsuma

had no need to fear as it turned out. Morris died of cancer shortly after closure, and never had to serve his time. Shortly after, Chuck acquired the classic 70s songs by Kool and The Gang including *Jungle Boogie, Get Down On It* and *Celebration* – along with the songs of KC and The Sunshine Band, which included such material as *That's The Way I Like It.*

Armed with an impressive catalogue of songs, one of their first projects was working with film director Bob Zemekis. He was famed for his work with *Back To The Future* and his then new project *Forrest Gump* starring Tom Hanks. Joel was hired as music supervisor – the person who selects all the tracks for the film – as well as compiler for the soundtrack album, featuring only classic American songs. Naturally, Joel was able to 'shoe in' plenty of Windswept compositions, about seven, in the 32-strong double album which went on to sell a phenomenal 12 million copies.

They started creating storylines for movies around song titles

Windswept was on its way! What followed was a craze by the movie industry to strongly identify music with films. This developed to such an extent that they started creating storylines for movies around song titles, such as *Pretty Woman, Stand By Me* and so on.

This was a golden time for Windswept. They kept on acquiring new catalogues and gave office room to many itinerant music supervisors, in return for them committing to include Windswept songs in their compilations whenever possible and for Windswept to receive a percentage of record royalties from the albums sold. What was quite revolutionary about Chuck's success in starting a new music publishing company was that he did it without signing any new writers, with the risk and attendant cost of advances and staff – just old songs. Many corporations have since used Chuck's model, but never with that kind of success.

So in spring 1993, Windswept opened the doors of its London office. My brief was to establish a high profile for the company,

Left to right: Yvonne Grace, Bob Grace, Nick Battle, Christian Ulf-Hansen

sign and develop unknown songwriters, and over all, make money. To do this, I needed some creative staff, and I hired a former acquaintance Nick Battle and a full-time financial controller Paul Flynn. Nick was also a Christian, so we decided to initiate a music industry Christian Union, which we called the Lamplighters. We trawled the UK industry for committed Christians, found

> **We decided to initiate a music industry Christian Union**

about ten, and started monthly meetings on Friday lunchtime at our offices. There, we prayed – among other things – for the prosperity of the company, and therefore our jobs! Later on, this prayer was spectacularly answered.

We also signed and developed some Christian songwriters. These included Chris Eaton, famous for his number one song for Cliff Richard, *Saviour's Day*, and Paul Field who also went on to write for Cliff. As our head office was strongly identified with movies, Nick suggested also hiring as a consultant Ivan Chandler, a UK music supervisor, in a bid to place our copyrights in UK movies and TV programmes. We soon discovered the UK movie industry is so small in comparison to the USA that this approach wouldn't work out.

| **Ivan gave us very valuable feedback about a new girl band called...'Spice'** |

However, Ivan did give us some very valuable feedback about a newly formed girl band. He thought they were great. They were called 'Spice'.

The Gold Badge Awards 2003:
Top row, left to right: Ben and Jonathan Finn, Guy Fletcher, Cliff Richard.
Bottom row, left to right: Peter Jenner, Bob Grace, Petula Clark, Midge Ure

Left to right: Bob Grace, Matt Redman

Thirteen

What You Really Really Want

I t wasn't a meeting. It was an invasion. Nothing could've prepared us for the energy unleashed around our Ikea-clad office when they arrived. 'Spice' had now become 'Spice Girls'. They all talked at once, manager Simon Fuller in a corner saying nothing, content to let the girls 'do their thing'. Our building was surrounded by double yellow lines, and Geri (Ginger Spice) had parked her tiny Fiat 500 right outside. To my horror, an aggressive traffic warden appeared, so I alerted Geri. Ginger Spice leant out of the window, and released a torrent of her persuasive powers loose on the unsuspecting warden, who meekly turned tail, and allowed the car to stay there, unticketed. That was the first and last time anyone got away with illegal parking in our mews.

I had plenty of experience in the past at China Records, dealing with groups who were demanding high advances to sign to the label. So I knew which questions to ask about justifying such requests. It was common for groups to demand in excess of £100,000 just to get their signatures on the dotted line, rather like footballers today. So when Simon and the girls announced they wanted an advance against future royalties of £200,000, I wasn't too fazed.

I merely wanted to know, as prospective partners in this venture, what they wanted this enormous amount of money for, and what were they going to spend it on. Investing in your career is one thing, but having such an advance to potentially squander it on riotous living is another! By this stage, although intrigued, I still hadn't heard a song, so enquired if this was possible.

A signal, by way of a knowing look, passed between the girls and Simon. They asked if I could push the table away to make some room. Nick and I duly complied, and was given a tape to play. This turned out to be a backing track with the vocals stripped off, for four or five of their songs. The moment I clicked 'play', the girls jumped into action, and Nick and I had our own, personal Spice Girls show, in our boardroom for the next 20 minutes. They were phenomenal, and I was blown away. They handed me a

Nick and I had our own personal Spice Girls show in our boardroom

cassette of five songs which turned out to be demos of the first few singles, and made their exit to Geri's Fiat – while Simon had a chauffeur waiting for him. I loved the tape and played it at home continuously.

My brief at Windswept was to discover and sign talent, and I knew this was a golden opportunity. I *Fedexed* copies of the tape to my immediate bosses in Tokyo and Los Angeles, preceded by exuberant phone calls. To be fair, they were both positive, and gave me the encouragement to proceed with negotiations, despite concerns about such a high advance for an unproven act. I rang Simon immediately, and told him we were all keen at Windswept. He told me he liked the idea of signing with us, as the marketing strategy of the group was to launch them in Japan first, three months ahead of the rest of the world. Being both Japanese owned and very proactive in press and promotion, Windswept could be vitally important to the success of their campaign.

The girls wanted to meet my Japanese boss, Ichirio Asatsuma, for themselves. I immediately rang him in Tokyo, and to his enduring credit, he jumped on a plane to London the following day.

At 11 o'clock the next Monday morning, Ichi (his nickname) and myself were in Simon's Battersea office called 19 Management. The girls duly arrived, and started to grill Ichi about his thoughts on their music. Companies so often fail at this crucial stage, with business-orientated executives knowing nothing about music, or how to communicate with artistes. Not Ichi, for he had lived with this tape, playing it over and over again on the long flight to London. Wouldn't you with £200,000 at risk!

Ichi gave the girls a taste of their own medicine, by singing to them in an excruciatingly awful voice, complete with Japanese accent, the verse and chorus of *Two Become One*. They were unprepared for this, and were absolutely thrilled. Again the nod happened between them and Simon, and there was another impromptu live performance from the girls. This was their trademark stunt, I later found out. It had been used time and time again in various degrees to impress people on their journey from being unknown hopefuls to getting the all-important record deal.

There seemed to be much acceptance between myself, Ichi, Simon and the girls, but I still had to make the deal. Ichi left immediately for the airport, and I went back to the office to ponder my next move. I rang Simon a couple of days later to check on the situation. He confirmed they had indeed signed to Virgin Records, and had three offers of 200K from major publishing companies on his desk. I reminded him how we had all gotten on so well at the meeting with Ichi, and asked what did I need to do to close the deal. He swiftly answered that an extra 50k would swing it. I said, 'I'll be right back'.

I figured the girls would either be massive – dwarfing such an advance very quickly – or a complete failure. I thought about the positives. There was a gap in the market for a female Take That, Simon was that rare find, a superb manager, Virgin was a great label, and the songs were terrific. This association had to be positive for Windswept, and success would put us on the map overnight.

I rang Ichi immediately, gave him the update, and reasoned with him we should go for it. To my delight he gave me the go ahead, and a few weeks later the deal was done. We signed the contract in the girls' lawyers' offices in Central London just before Christmas in 1994.

That wasn't the only momentous occasion concerning girls that happened that year. On February 22nd my beautiful daughter, Anna, was born in a hospital near Guildford. We chose this hospital, even though we lived in Chelsea, as the

> **My beautiful daughter Anna was born in a hospital near Guildford**

consultant who had a practice in Chelsea, was actually based in a Guildford hospital. It was also quite handy for Adrian to come and visit his new sister, as he was a boarder at nearby Cranleigh School.

A minor problem that needed overcoming was that our house didn't have a bedroom for Anna, and we'd utilised all the extension possibilities already. There was a very small room, which just about accommodated her cot, so we had a few months' breathing space to consider our options. The cost of upscaling in Chelsea was enormous, and I had long wanted to move slightly out of London.

Wimbledon was a delightful place to raise a family – six miles from the centre of London, but with a countrified feel due to the proximity of the common. We found a large house and garden, quarter of a mile from the common and went for it, moving there in May 1994. Life was good. We started attending a local congregation called Queens Road Baptist Church, which was experiencing a time of spiritual renewal. Dubbed by the press the 'Toronto Blessing' – as it started at a church in Canada – this movement drew people from far and wide.

My father Sydney had been in a nursing home for about a year due to recurring panic attacks. In June 1996, he had a fall in the shower there, which resulted in a fractured hip that had to be replaced. By the beginning of July he was out of hospital and convalescing. The coming July 4th was going to be a big day. It was my parents' 60th (diamond) wedding anniversary. So I drove down to Angmering-on-Sea, with my sister Virginia, collected my mother, Eunice, and we went on together to visit Dad in the nearby nursing home for the celebration. We spent a wonderful, loving afternoon together as a family, with many cuddles, cakes and kind words. I remember massaging Dad's legs which were painful at that time as a result of his operation. The only negative thing was that Dad would shout out very loud when he had a panic attack.

'Oh God, oh Christ,' he cried on this occasion, 'help me.'

'Shut up, Sydney,' the other patients shouted back.

This was coming from a man who although sweet natured and of exemplary character, didn't know God, despite my efforts to influence him. He once threw a Gideon's Bible across the hospital ward when I was attempting to share its message with him. I didn't think too much of this at the time, as it was fairly usual behaviour, sadly. We took Mother home, and returned to London.

The following morning back in Wimbledon, about 11 am, I was thinking about Dad when I had the sensation of being punched hard in the stomach. I was literally brought to my knees, and felt God was very near. I felt strongly urged to pray for my father right then, but for what I was not sure, as he seemed relatively fine when I had left him the previous day. I called Yvonne in, and told her I felt something bad was happening to Dad, and we both prayed until we felt at peace again.

> **I was literally brought to my knees, and felt God was very near**

I had just dropped off to sleep that night, when a nurse from a Worthing hospital rang to tell me my father had just died. Apparently, he suffered a mild heart attack the following morning after the visit, which intensified during the day, and was admitted to hospital. No one informed my family of this development, which didn't surprise me as it was partly due to the negligence of the nursing home's staff that he fell in the shower in the first place. However, God obviously knew, which is why I believe he prompted me to pray so sharply. To be honest, I can't remember what I prayed for, as I was pretty distressed at that time. Our church's pastor Norman Moss came over to our house the day after. He believed Dad was in safe hands in heaven.

'Everyone who calls on the name of the Lord will be saved,' he quoted from the Old Testament book of Joel.

That's exactly what my Dad had been shouting two days earlier. Norman further assured me from his experience of being a pastor for over 30 years that he had seen this happen time and again. I realised Dad had locked into God's rescue plan for his soul – just as I had for myself – and just as any of us can, if we want to.

Bob Grace and The Spice Girls
© Doug McKenzie Photography

Fourteen

Whole Again

The Spice Girls' UK launch came about the same time as the upheaval at home. They had made a big impression in Japan, as planned. Now came the release of their debut single *Wannabe* co-written between the girls and their producers, Matt Rowe and Richard Stannard. It shot up the charts like a rocket, selling eventually an astonishing six million copies worldwide.

| I realised Dad had locked into God's rescue plan

It went to number one in 31 countries – including the USA – where it stayed at number one for a month in January 1997. They became a phenomenon, selling more than 50 million albums and becoming the world's most successful girl band ever. What an answer to the prayers we had prayed in our office that day. The impact also on my career was enormous. I have to admit, I enjoyed my day in the sun.

About a year before the Spice Girls split up, EMI Music Publishing bought most of Windswept Music for a sum in excess of $200 million. We were able to keep trading, however, as Windswept 2, as certain ongoing contracts were excluded from the acquisition. With some of the funding from the deal, Windswept US bought another big song catalogue, and I had some funds available to invest in new UK talent. Nick Battle went his own way at that time, and we trimmed the UK company down a little. Peter McCamley now became my number two, and he alerted me to an emerging artist named Craig David.

Despite intense competition from rival companies, Craig signed with us, and enjoyed enormous success internationally. His debut album *Born To Do It* went on to sell seven million albums, and he had numerous hit singles. We also invested in the songwriting/production team around Atomic Kitten, who also enjoyed big success. Their single *Whole Again* was number one for a month in England and also in Germany. With ongoing hits from Albert Hammond and Burt Bacharach's songs – which were still licensed to us – we continued to prosper.

However, I could see the writing on the wall, and the future for the music industry looked bleak. A combination of illegal 'free' downloads of songs from the Internet, kids bluetoothing songs on their mobiles to each other, and the soaring cost of deals and overheads were having a devastating impact on the profitability of the company. This came to a head for me, when an emerging group called 'Busted' came to see me. They played an acoustic impromptu gig for me in my office, and I thought they were great. I was well poised to make a deal as one of my writers, Wee John, was involved with putting Busted together, and was writing and producing with them. However, the advance and terms their managers and lawyers demanded were unrealistic from my point of view.

Left to right: Bob Grace, Craig David, Peter McCamley

I couldn't recommend the deal to my head office, so I declined, taking some comfort in the fact that I had about 20 per cent of the songs of the album anyway, due to Wee John's involvement. As we all know, they went on to be massive for a while. Rather than being thrilled that at least I had some participation in their success, I was perturbed that the purpose for Windswept's existence in the UK was basically redundant.

My goal was to spot, and sign and develop unknown talent. If such deals didn't make financial sense, even if the act became successful, then there was no point in carrying on. The critical point was that it was crucial to have a long term right to the songs' earnings. The maximum rights under English law were for a duration of 70 years, following the death of the last surviving writer. The deal norm at this time, even for unknowns, was a maximum of seven years' retention of the copyrights, following the end of the deal. This figure doesn't wash when evaluating publishing companies for possible purchase, the minimum period for such evaluations being ten years.

I soldiered on for a while, understandably keeping my thoughts to myself for obvious reasons of survival. However, it came as no real surprise in June 2003 when the US office started the process of 'shuttering' the UK operation, starting with the highest overhead – me! They reasoned, correctly, that their investment dollars were no longer viable in the UK market, and they'd be better served by investments in their own country. They didn't initiate this policy as it was being acted out through numerous firms already, but they just stepped in line. I only know of a handful of wholly owned UK subsidiaries of US music publishing companies in operation today, as I write.

With the assistance of John Benedict, a most able music industry lawyer and buddy, I explored joint venture situations with all the major companies – but to no avail. My track record would've previously attracted investors clamouring to be involved, but market conditions had changed dramatically. Unperturbed, I formed my own music publishing company, Bay Songs Ltd, with business partner Iqbal, an unchallenged genius in copyright and royalty administration, and signed an unknown folk singer called Karine Polwart. She went on to achieve great things in her field, scooping song of the year with *The Sun's Coming Over The Hill* and album of the year with *Faultlines* at the prestigious BBC Radio 2 Folk Awards, in February 2005. Although these awards were extremely gratifying for both Karine and myself, they didn't bring even close the financial rewards of my previous successes.

My old friend Derek Green came by our house for a meal. He told me our previous boss and A&M Records co-founder Jerry Moss had been asked if he would ever return to the industry. His response was that he couldn't return to an industry that was unrecognisable to him. That was exactly how I felt about it all in 2005. I didn't identify with the talent or the business. The business model had radically changed. Record companies stimulated by the plethora of 'reality TV' shows had morphed into advertising agencies,

> **The blight of celebrity status was polluting the industry**

branding artists like products. The blight of celebrity status was polluting the industry, with Andy Warhol's prediction in the 1960s coming true – 'everyone will be a star for 15 minutes'.

It's no longer necessary to master an instrument or be able to sing, as technology can assist them. An eye-catching image and attitude are crucial. Overnight success can be crafted by expert manipulation of the Internet. While not saying this is wholly wrong, I do have to say, in the words of the 'dragons' in the den – 'I'm out!' It's no longer an industry that holds any appeal to me. I attend a few events, as it's great to catch up with old friends. After more than 40 years in a business that was also a lifestyle, I have some cherished friendships. It's also a great opportunity to model the hope of the Christian life to others.

We sold up in Wimbledon in the summer of 2005, and moved west to the beautiful city of Bath. Great schools, great Christian ministries, lovely countryside and friendly people all contribute to a superb place to live. If only it wasn't so hilly! I'm now a partner in a mailing house in Cornwall with three great guys, Steve Double, Stuart Taylor and Nick Mayo. We're all Christians, and are delighted that the vision of the company – to provide employment in an area of rank joblessness – is working well despite the recession. We're now in our seventh year, creating jobs for at least 60 people.

I became an active member of the Healing On The Streets Ministry in Bath, founded by Paul Skelton, and legendary Christian speaker Don Latham is encouraging me to follow in his footsteps.

With the 'empty nest' approaching in a few months when Anna goes off to university, Yvonne and I are considering where we go and what we do in the future. We've downsized from our rurally based home to something smaller and more manageable nearer to the city, and we'll probably spend much more time in the US were Yvonne has a large family. I have a longstanding desire and dream to eventually complete my studies with a Bible School in Colorado and hope Yvonne will join me.

Yvonne, James and Bob Grace in the Philippines

The church in the Philippines, where my son James had worked, was completed in summer 2011. Yvonne and I went out for the grand opening. Our friend Malcolm, a builder, used to go regularly on mission to this village, Kinuman, to help rebuild dilapidated houses. On one visit, he met a local girl, Meme, who was to become his wife. She had long nursed a dream to replace the shack which served as a church with a purpose-built brick building. We, along with many others, have helped in bringing this dream into reality. It has attracted many young locals, and recently Malcolm baptised over 45 people in the sea. We had a wonderful experience of mission during our week there for the opening. We preached at the new church and at the home congregation named The Happy Church, led a marriage seminar, participated in a crusade, saw miraculous healings and was able to preach and sing at a Bible College and a prison. Malcolm now lives there full-time, where he has become a builder of Kingdom, and along with Meme is regularly discipling and encouraging people.

All I can say is that Jesus has done some great things for me in my life. My school reports over the years would continually say I was insecure and immature. After turning my back on religion, and Jesus in particular for over 40 years, he turned me round overnight in the summer of 1988. Now he is my rock – the foundation of my life. Jesus was able **Jesus has done some great things for me in my life** to accomplish something that none of the self-help programmes could deal with. He changed me from the inside out. Like the title of the hit song I published in 1987, *Something Inside So Strong*, that's what he's put in me.

As a boy I declared that I would walk in my earthly father's footsteps as a career choice. Now since 1988, I have walked in my Heavenly Father's footsteps. He promises to be a lamp to my path and a light to my feet (Psalm 119:105).

At the time of writing I have been delivered from bowel cancer. At no time from the unexpected diagnosis to post recovery have I had to succumb to fear...His perfect peace has protected me. I've been greatly encouraged by a line from one of the Psalms which says, *'I will send forth my word and heal you and deliver you from all your destructions'* (Psalm 107:20).

Thank you, Jesus.

From left to right: Adrian, Bob, Anna, Yvonne

Rock Solid

Epilogue

I have proved to myself that Jesus is alive and well. He's not just a figure from well-documented history, but also a living person who is ready and willing to help us – 24/7.

Sadly, I chose him as a last resort. That doesn't have to be so for everyone else. The earlier we choose him, the better our lives will be. So I would urge everyone to get to know Jesus now. As reflected in this book's title, your life will become 'Rock Solid' if you place your trust on Him.

The easiest way is to join an introductory course to Christianity. There are several of these running at churches and community centres up and down the country. I recommend *Alpha*, but you may find a different course near you.

I also heartily recommend Andrew Wommack's ministry. I've attended his Bible college, and consider him the finest Bible teacher I've ever heard. There's lots of free stuff, and wonderful information on his website, www.awmi.net

I also highly recommend Kenneth and Gloria Copelands' ministry. Their website is www.kcm.org.uk. And if my story helps you, please let me know. You can contact me at: bob@rocksolidthebook.co.uk and www.rocksolidthebook.co.uk

Find the Lord now. I guarantee it will be the best investment you'll ever make. And, of course, God is always there. He'll never leave you or forsake you, so just call on him, anyway. Just like I did. Just like my dad did.

Call on the name of the Lord.